Forex Trading

Complete Beginners Guide to Learn the Best Swing and Day Trading Strategies, Tools, Generate Passive Income and Market Psychology on Currency Pairs

Jim Douglas

© **Copyright 2019 by ___Jim Douglas___ -
All rights reserved.**

This document is geared towards providing exact and reliable information in regards to the topic and issue covered. The publication is sold with the idea that the publisher is not required to render accounting, officially permitted, or otherwise, qualified services. If advice is necessary, legal or professional, a practiced individual in the profession should be ordered.

- From a Declaration of Principles which was accepted and approved equally by a Committee of the American Bar Association and a Committee of Publishers and Associations.

In no way is it legal to reproduce, duplicate, or transmit any part of this document in either electronic means or in printed format. Recording of this publication is strictly prohibited and any storage of this document is not allowed unless with written permission from the publisher. All rights reserved.

The information provided herein is stated to be truthful and consistent, in that any liability, in terms of inattention or otherwise, by any usage or abuse of any policies, processes, or directions contained within is the solitary and utter responsibility of the recipient reader. Under no circumstances will any legal responsibility or blame be held against the publisher for any reparation, damages, or monetary loss due to the information herein, either directly or indirectly.

Respective authors own all copyrights not held by the publisher.

The information herein is offered for informational purposes solely, and is universal as so. The presentation of the information is without contract or any type of guarantee assurance.

The trademarks that are used are without any consent, and the publication of the trademark is without permission or backing by the trademark owner. All trademarks and brands within this book are for clarifying purposes only and are the owned by the owners themselves, not affiliated with this document.

Table of Contents

Introduction 1

Chapter 1: WHAT IS FOREX TRADING? 13

    Concepts of forex trading 15

    IMPORTANCE OF FOREX TRADING 21

    ADVANTAGES OF TRADING FOREX 25

Chapter 2: ANALYZING THE FINANCIAL MARKETS 33

    FUNDAMENTAL ANALYSIS 35

    TECHNICAL ANALYSIS 51

    CURRENCY FORECASTING - WHAT BOOKWORMS ECONOMISTS LOOK AT 67

Chapter 3: THE NEED TO BE OBJECTIVE 77

    STEP-BY-STEP SECRETS TO WIN WITH FOREX 80

    DANGERS OF GETTING EMOTIONAL ABOUT FOREX TRADE 85

Chapter 4: FOREX TRADING STRATEGY 89

    CHANNEL BREAKOUT 90

    THE IMPORTANCE OF REAL POWER STRATEGY 91

    THE ADVANTAGES OF AUTOMATED FOREX TRADING 97

CALCULATING INTEREST ON FOREX TRADES 98

Chapter 5: FOREX TRADING PSYCHOLOGY .. 101

PSYCHOLOGY OF A SUCCESSFUL TRADER IN THE FOREX MARKET 106

MASS PSYCHOLOGY AND ITS MEASURES ... 111

Chapter 6: MONEY AND POSITION MANAGEMENT 117

TRADING JOURNAL 126

RISK MANAGEMENT 131

Chapter 7: CURRENCY FUTURES AND CRYPTOCURRENCIES 143

WHAT ARE CURRENCY FUTURES? 143

CRYPTOCURRENCIES 146

WHY TRADE WITH CRYPTOCURRENCIES? .. 150

HOW TO TRADE CRYPTOCURRENCIES 152

BEST CRYPTOCURRENCIES FOR TRADING .. 155

Chapter 8: INFORMATION ON RISK 165

How to manage risks in currency trade? 166

Tools and tips for risk management 170

Conclusion 175

Introduction

The foreign exchange market, or Forex market, is a fast-paced and exciting market. Until recently, this kind of trading was only done by central banks, corporations, financial institutions, and wealthy individuals. But thanks to the emergence of the internet, many more people can join the market and use it to do investing as well.

Daily currency fluctuations are going to be small. Most pairs of currencies are only going to move about a cent each day, which will represent a change that is less than 1 percent in the value of the currency. This means that in most cases, the Forex market is going to be one of the least volatile financial markets around. Therefore, many currency speculators are going to rely on enormous amounts of leverage to increase how valuable a potential movement can be. In fact, with the Forex market, the leverage can be as high as 250:1.

This leverage is really high and can be really risky. But because of the deep amount of liquidity and the fact that the Forex market is available to be traded around the clock, many brokers can make high leverage the standard of the industry which can make the movements more meaningful for most currency traders.

Extreme liquidity and the high leverage of this market have really helped to push rapid growth in the market, making it a great place for investing with many traders. Positions on this market can be opened, and then closed again, within minutes, or the trader can choose to hold onto the position for months. Currency prices are going to be based on the idea of supply and demand or that currency pair at the time, and it is hard to manipulate them easily, simply because the size of the market is just so big. Even central banks and other large players in the market are not able to make changes that will move the prices of currency pairs as well.

While many of the players in the Forex market are going to be larger players like banks and financial institutions, there are still opportunities for investors to get in. However, for the individual to do well, they need to know some of the basics of any movements in the currency, or they are going to run into trouble and will lose more money than they can gain on this market.

If you live in the United States and you wish to buy some cheese from France, for example, either you or the company that you purchase the cheese from will need to pay for that product using euros.

This means that the importer in the United States would have to take their USD and then exchange it out for euros so that they can pay for the cheese (or any other product depending on what they work on. The same will go for traveling and so much more. If you wish to leave the United States and go to Egypt, you will have to change your money into the one that is the locally accepted currency before you can purchase anything there.

The need to exchange these currencies is one of the biggest reasons why this is the largest and the most liquid financial market in the world. It is so huge because it has to deal with all the currencies that are present in the world. It is estimated that the average value that is traded on this forum is $2,000 billion each day (based on the USD). The total volume is going to change each day though, and it is likely that this number will keep going up.

One unique aspect of this particular market is that there isn't a central marketplace for this exchange. Instead, the currency is going to be conducted electronically over the counter. What this means is that all of the transactions that occur with the Forex market is going to occur via computers and between traders that are around the world, rather than with one centralized exchange like what happens with the stock market.

The Forex market is going to be open 24 hours a day, five and a half days a week, and the currencies can be traded at all the financial centers throughout the world. With so many different countries on the market, it is possible that the market is starting brand new in Hong Kong and Tokyo when it is ending for the day with the United States. This is why the Forex market has the potential to be active at any time of the day, and the price quotes on currencies are likely to change all of the time.

These include the spot market, the futures market, and the forwards market. The forex trading with the spot market is often the largest because it is the underlying real asset that the futures and the forwards market are based on. Traditionally, the futures market was the most popular because it stayed open for longer times with individual investors. But thanks to electronic trading and more Forex brokers, more people have started to go with the spot market.

The spot market is where the currencies are going to be bought or sold based on their current price. The price that you can buy or sell the currencies at will be determined by supply and demand and can reflect a lot of different things including political situations, economic performance, interest rates, and more.

This is going to be a bilateral transaction where one party is going to deliver an amount for the currency that is agreed upon to the counterparty, and then they will receive a specified amount of another currency at the exchange rate value. After the position is closed, the settlement is going to be in cash. Although this is the market that is known for dealing with transactions that happen in the present, rather than in the future, it does take about two days for the settlement to get done.

But with the futures market, contracts are going to be bought and then sold based on a standard size and settlement date and will occur on the market for public commodities. For these, the National Futures Association in the United States will regulate this kind of market. These contracts are going to have more specifics with them, including how many units the parties will trade, the delivery as well as the settlement dates, the minimum price increments, and more. These all need to be determined ahead of time to make sure everyone is on the same page.

Both of these contracts are binding, and they will also be settled for cash. They have expiration dates, but you can buy and sell the contracts before that date as well. The forwards and the futures markets are a great way to add in some protection against any risks when doing trades on the Forex market.

There are a lot of benefits of working in the Forex market, which makes it the perfect choice when you are looking for new investment to help you out. Some of the benefits that come with trading in the Forex market include:

• It is open 24-hours a day: This is a worldwide trading platform, which means that there is going to be a market open somewhere, even if it's not in your own country.

• High Liquidity: Liquidity is the ability of any asset to quickly be converted over into cash, without a price discount. What this means in Forex is that you can move your money into and out of the market with very little price movement.

• Costs for the transactions are low: The cost of a transaction will often be put into the price with Forex, and it is known as the spread. The spread will be the difference between your purchase and your selling price. Having lower costs for transactions can do wonders when it comes to helping you to save money and put more of your profits on investment back into your pocket.

- You can use leverage: Forex brokers do allow their traders to use leverage. Leverage is basically the ability to trade some extra money on the market than what you have in your account. This helps you to make some bigger trades but can be risky to accomplish as well.
- This means that if you look at the market and you think that a currency pair is going to increase over time, you can purchase it or decide to go long. If you think that this value is going to decrease, you can either sell it or go short.
- Lots of options: If you are first looking at the Forex market, it is likely that you will see a lot of options available. You can pick from a wide variety of currency pairs. And while many people feel like they should stick with some of the major pairs when they first get started to help them gain familiarity with the market, it is also possible to try out some different matches of currency pairs based on what you read in the market and what interest you the most. Everyone can join the Forex market and see some success simply

because there are so many options and it is possible to earn money no matter where the currencies go, as long as you made the right predictions.

These are just some of the benefits that can come with working in the Forex market. There are also a few negatives that you will need to watch out for. For example, while the Forex market is one that is open 24-hours a day, this can also be a negative because a short move may happen when you aren't able to watch the screen. No one can sit around and watch the market all the time so this can lead to some positions not going the way that you want. You need to make sure that you pick currencies that will stay stable, even overnight, because no one can watch the market all the time.

Also, while the transaction costs are going to be lower on this market compared to others, there can be issues if you end up trading too much. If you trade all the time, the costs are still going to add up, and they may not be enough to help you see the results that you want or cover the profits as they should. For the most part, it is best to go with a long-term investing strategy because you only have to pay for the transactions once and then you can enjoy the profits when it is time to take out.

Before you enter the market, make sure that both of the currencies in your currency pair are liquid enough. If one currency pair doesn't have the right amount of liquidity, it can become very difficult to sell that position later on. The more liquidity that both of the currencies have in your pair, the easier it is to buy and sell them and do your trades.

Always watch out for the idea of leverage. Yes, this does allow you to have a stronger position when you enter because you get to work with more capital than you would in other situations. But this can be a really dangerous mindset to get into. Using more capital than you have to do a trade can increase your risk and may make it, so you lose a ton of money. Until you become more familiar with the Forex market, it is best to just stick with the capital that you can afford to lose, rather than relying on leverage. This helps you make strong and sound decisions, without going over your head.

There is so much to love about the Forex market. There are many different currency pairs that you can work with, the market is open all the time, there are many ways to make profits, and so much more. This is definitely a type of investment that can work out well for many investors, whether they are more advanced or just getting started.

Chapter 1: WHAT IS FOREX TRADING?

Forex (Foreign Exchange Market) is the biggest financial market in the world. Therefore, Forex trading refers to Currency exchange trading. As you know, it is extremely important for currencies to exist in this world. Without them, people will not be able to buy and sell goods. Now, these goods will not always be bought and sold in the local country alone and will also have to be bought from a foreign country. Now say for example your line in Germany and wish to buy a laptop from China. The German currency is Euro, and Chinese currency is Yuan. Now, when you wish to buy the laptop, the Chinese seller will most likely not accept the Euro as payment, but would accept Dollars, as up until now, Dollars is the most widely accepted currency and easy to convert into Yuan as he will want the Yuan, which is the ultimately currency he will want in his bank account in China. So, you will have to exchange your Euro for Dollars to pay the Chinese seller. Here, you have to understand that the currency will get converted to certain "Exchange rate" quoted by the market at the time the conversion occurs. This "rate" will always be a difference in the values of the currencies. This difference will always prove to be an advantage for one country and a disadvantage to another in ways that we could analyze in the future.

Now say 1 Euro is valued at 20 Yuan. This means that the German trader can exchange 1 Euro for 20 Yuan and 100 Euro for 2000 Yuan. Here, the Yuan trails the Euro, which means that Germany is in a better place in terms of forex trading. On the other hand, if a trader in China were to buy wine from Germany then he would have to pay a lot more towards it due to the difference in rates between the two currencies. This is just an example, and the difference in rates can be quite different from this. It can be higher or lower in value.

Now here, a buyer wanted to exchange the money because they wished to buy something from a foreign seller, but Forex is not always traded for this reason alone. It is also traded to capitalize upon the difference in values. You could be able to make big profits if you play the game right, but there are certain things that you must learn about first in order to invest in the Forex market.

Through the course of this book, we will look in detail at how you can do so. In this next segment, we will look at the basic concepts of forex trading.

Concepts of forex trading

The majors

The very first concept that you must understand is the majors. The majors refer to the major currencies that are regularly traded in the Forex market. The stock market has thousands of shares that the trader can choose from to invest in. This more often than not ends up confusing the trader and might also cause them to make the wrong investments. But this problem is tackled in the Forex market, as there are certain major currencies that you can trade in on a regular basis. These are based on trends and after understanding which countries provide you with the best overvalued and undervalued advantages. Here is the list of the 8 major countries that you can turn to in order remain with the highest profit.

The United States of America

Canada

Europe

United Kingdom

Switzerland

Australia

New Zealand

Japan

These countries and their currencies are identified as the big 8 because they have the best financial markets and/or manufacturing capabilities. These facts allow their currencies to always remain in demand for exchange. If you exchange any of these currencies in the right moment, your investment will surely be safe. For that, you have to constantly follow the economic scene of all the individual countries.

Buy and sell

You have to understand that the Forex market works in a simultaneous buying and selling fashion. This means that if you want to buy one currency, you will have to sell the one you have at the same time. This is easy to understand if you have, for example, physical Euros, and walk into a Bank and exchange for physical Dollars. You sell your Euros and purchased Dollars. One transaction that includes buy and sell.

But in the Forex world, we trade Forex symbols called "pairs." So, when you are buying one currency, you will automatically be selling another. In the simple example mentioned above, you traded the pair EUR/USD. In a trading platform, you use this symbol if you want to buy Euros (in Dollars) or Dollars (in Euros). All pairs or symbols have the same principle. If you "buy the symbol" you are buying the first currency if you "sell the symbol" you are buying the second currency. You have to get used to this concept in order to trade in Forex. You will have to calculate the basis points of the currencies based on their difference. That you can calculate by looking at the trending rates of the two currencies. The basis points refer to a measure of the interest or any percentages that you need to calculate before you go ahead with a deal. You will be able to calculate your gain by doing so.

Rate of return

The rate of return in the forex market is quite large. This means that you can remain with a big profit or a big loss depending on your investment. There have been cases of people making millions by just investing a few hundred or thousand dollars. This is possible if you know to invest in the market the right way. Let's say you invest $10 in the market and it gives you a return of $1000. That is highly possible in the currency market. However, if you get it wrong, then you might end up losing a lot of money. The currency market is extremely volatile, and you have to remain abreast of the difference in values of the currencies. The idea is to look for currencies that are momentarily undervalued, that way, you can expect a big change in value to finally close the transaction at your desired profit. If at any time you feel that the prices of the currencies are going to cause you a loss, then you must sell them off.

Dual benefits

The forex market offers you dual benefits when you invest in the market. It is better known as the Currency Carry Trade. The Currency Carry Trade is one where the person stands to benefit in two ways. Let us look at an example. Now let's say a Chinese trader exchanges 5000 Yuan for dollars and buys a bond with the dollars' worth. The trader will receive an interest of 5% on the bond provided the rate of exchange between the two countries remains the same. If it does, then the trader will stand to gain a profit of 50% owing to the difference in the currency values. This is an added benefit to the fact that the trader will also be able to avail a profit from selling the bond later. Here, you have to understand that the exchange rate between the two should remain the same otherwise the trader will lose money. This risk is quite high with currencies whose rates are quite volatile. You will not be able to predict the difference in rates, and by the time you withdraw from it, you probably would have lost quite some money. The difference in the rates usually occurs over a period of years and will not be within a short period of time.

OTC

Unlike the regular Stock Market (that deals with regulated Financial Instruments), Forex is always traded OTC (over the counter). This means that the currencies are not considered "financial instruments" in most countries and are not regulated as such. Banks and Brokers trade currencies via an Electronic Communication Network (ECN). A medium that is different from a stock market exchange like NYSE or AMEX. A dealer will be responsible for the trade, and there will be no centralized control over the trade. It is the same manner in which penny stocks and bonds are exchanged. You will have to do some homework on how you can start trading in your local market as the method differs from country to country. You have to look at dealers that will help you get these currencies. All Banks and Brokers, authorized to exchange, are connected to this network. In essence, you need an authorized bank or broker to handle your orders via the internet.

These form the different basic concepts of forex that you have to understand if you wish to trade in it. They will act as your guide when you partake in forex trading.

IMPORTANCE OF FOREX TRADING

At the core of Forex, you are dealing with currency trading. And at the core of that currency trading, you have speculation about the values of currencies.

Hold on, you say.

Speculation? You ask. Didn't you tell me not to assume anything? Now you are telling me to go ahead and speculate?

Of course, you are going to speculate. But before we get to that, let us cover some of the basics first.

Currency trading is speculation. It is as simple as that. You are using what knowledge and information you have to make a profit by buying currencies. It is like buying stocks or any other financial security; you make a transaction and hope to make a profitable return on it. However, in the Forex market, the securities you are dealing with concern the currencies of nations.

But in the world of Forex, speculation is not based on blind assumptions. It is not even gambling (even though some people might think that it is so). When you gamble or make a guess, you are playing with your money even though you know that the odds are against you. You just hope that, given time, lady luck will smile at you with teeth so white that you could use them as floodlights. Typically, when you invest, you are aiming to minimize the risks and maximize the return over a certain period of time (usually months or years). In Forex, you are maximizing returns over a short period of time (usually minutes, hours, or days). This involves speculating (or also known as "active trading" in the Forex world) where you adopt calculated financial risks in order to gain a profit.

And there you have the keyword that comes into play when describing Forex: calculated. You are not just sitting blindly twiddling your thumbs hoping to make it rich. You are going to read the trends, understand the shifts, and even use the latest news to make calculated risks.

The best way to understand your actions is by taking the example of a business. If you are the owner of a business, then you are going to be making calculated risks. Should you increase the available stock that you have? Do you want to hire more employees? Should you think about expanding your business or opening a branch in another location? Do you need to spend heavily on big marketing campaigns?

You may never be certain about the outcomes of any of those decisions. But you do make choices based on the information you have. For example, you notice that there is a demand for your products in another state. After conducting a market survey, you decide that it would be profitable for you to have a branch in that state. You immediately open up another business.

But what if you are not receiving profits that way you had expected? What are you going to do then? Are you going to pack up and call it quits? Or will you try some other tactics to attract customers to your business?

It is the same with Forex. When you speculate, you are making decisions about your investment based on the information you have with you.

This is why not many people realize before venturing into Forex that they need to be equipped with a certain frame of mind and skill set.

- You need to be dedicated. You can invest in the Forex market and ignore it for a few days, but then you must return to it to make a few changes.

- You need to have financial and technological resources. Even though you can start small, you are not going to last long if all you have is lunch money. When it comes to technological resources, you need to make sure that you have a steady access to the internet and the trading platform.

- You need to have financial discipline. You do not need to have a finance degree. Rather, you should be capable of understanding trends and numbers.

- You need to be emotionally strong. Things do not always go your way. But some of the biggest successes in Forex happen because people do not get emotional over their trades. They figure out ways to bounce back.

- You need to have the perseverance to always seek out new information, new ways to manage your risk, and look for new opportunities.

- Finally, you should be a sponge, able to absorb knowledge about the politics, economics, and market situations of a particular country. That means it is time to renew your newspaper subscriptions.

ADVANTAGES OF TRADING FOREX

There are many benefits to trading in forex markets. Let us look at some of them in this chapter.

Liquidity

The first and most important benefit of forex trading is its liquidity. As you know, the forex market is extremely liquid meaning you can sell your currency at any time. There will be a lot of takers for it, as they will be looking to buy the particular currency. The highly liquid market can help you avoid any loss as you don't have to wait on your currency to be sold.

And all of it is automatic. You only have to give the sell order, and within no time your entire order will be sold.

Timing

The forex market is open 24 hours a day, which makes it a great place to invest at. You can keep trading during the day and also during the night if you are dealing with a country's currency whose day timings coincide with your night timings. You can come up with a schedule that will allow you to conveniently trade with all of the different countries that lie in the different time zones. You can also quickly sell off a bad currency without having to wait the whole night or day.

Returns

The rate of returns in foreign currency trade is quite high. You will see that it is possible for you to invest just $10 and control as much as $1000 with it. All you have to do is look for the best currency pairs and start buying and selling them. We looked at the 8 majors in a previous chapter, and you have to look at their rates and trade in them. The leverage that these investments provide is always on the higher side, which makes them an ideal investment avenue for both beginners and old hands.

Costs

The transaction costs of this type of trade are very low. You don't have to worry about big fees when you buy and sell foreign currencies. That is the one big concern that most stock traders have, as they will worry about having to shell out a lot of money towards transaction costs. But that worry is eliminated in currency exchanges, and you can save on quite a lot of money just by choosing to invest in currency.

Non-directional trade

The forex market follows a non-directional trade. This means that it does not matter if the difference in the currencies is going upwards or downwards, you will always have the chance to remain with a profit. This is mostly because there is scope for you to short a deal or go long on it depending on the situation and rate of difference. You will understand how this works as and when you partake in it. The main aim of investing in forex is to remain with a steady profit, which is only possible if you know when to hold on to an investment and when to sell it off. This very aspect is seen as being a buffer by traders and is the main reason for them choosing to invest in forex.

Middlemen eliminated

With forex trade, it is possible for you to eliminate any middlemen. These middlemen will unnecessarily charge you a fee and your costs with keep piling up. So, you can easily avoid these unnecessary costs and increase your profit margin. These middlemen need not always be brokers and can also be other people who will simply get in the way of your trade just to make a quick buck out of it. You have to be careful and stave such people off in order to avoid any unnecessary costs that they will bring about. Education is key here and the more you know, the better your chances of avoiding any such frauds.

No unfair trade

There is n0 possibility of anyone rich investor controlling the market. This is quite common in the stock market where a single big investor will end up investing a lot of money in a particular stock and then withdraw from it quickly and affect the market negatively. This is not a possibility in the foreign currency market as there is no scope for a single large trader to dominate the market. These traders will all belong to different countries, and it will not be possible for them to control the entire market as a whole. There will be free trade, and you can make the most use of it.

No entry barrier

There is no entry barrier, and you can enter and exit the market at any time you like. There is also no limit on the investment amount that you can enter with. As was mentioned earlier, you can invest something as big as $10,000 or as small as $10 and control the market. You have to try and diversify your currency investments in a way that you minimize your risk potential and increase your profit potential. You can start out with a small sum and then gradually increase it as you go.

Certainty

There is a certain certainty attached with foreign currencies. You will have the chance to avail guaranteed profits if you invest in currency pairs that are doing well. These can be surmised by going through all the different currency pairs that are doing well in the market. With experience, you will be able to cut down on your losses with ease and also increase your profits. You have to learn from your experience and ensure that you know exactly what you are doing.

Easy information

Information on the topic of foreign currencies is easily available on the internet and from other sources. This information can be utilized to invest in the best currency pairs. You have to do a quick search of which two pairs are doing well and invest in them without wasting too much time. If you need any other information on the topic, then this book will guide you through it. You can directly go to the topic that you seek and look at the details to provide there.

Apart from these, there are certain other benefits like minimal commission charged by the OTC agent and instant execution of your market orders. No agency will be able to control the foreign exchange market.

These form the different benefits of trading in the forex market but are not limited to just these. You will be acquainted with the others as and when you start investing in it.

Chapter 2: ANALYZING THE FINANCIAL MARKETS

The many economies of the world are in a constant state of flux. You now know where to look to find out where in a cycle they currently are – and make trading decisions accordingly – but what do those cycles actually mean?

When boiled down to the basics, an economy is either going to be in a time of expansion or a time of recession. In the former case, there is an increase in economic activity and gross domestic product, which means more disposable income and thus spending, better employment levels and more demand.

A recession is basically the opposite and will see a drop in economic activity that has a blanket effect across internal markets for such things as housing and labor. If this gets bad enough or goes on for long enough, it becomes known as a depression.

Within those cycles you'll find inflation and deflation. Inflation refers to the prices being charged for items and services and usually rises when there is more demand than supply. Deflation, once again, is its opposite.

Gross domestic product refers to the overall value of those items and services that a single country generates over the course of one year. It's what the central banks tend to use to analyze the growth of the economy, which means it's also the best place to look to find out whether that country's economy is on the rise or on the decline.

It represents how much consumers are consuming, how much investment and government spending is going on and how much exporting is taking place.

Meanwhile, the "balance of payments" can tell you how healthy the economy is in comparison to others in the world, and it can do so fairly directly. It refers to all international activities and is considered to be in a good state when the country is accepting more payments from other countries than it is making.

The financial account will tell you how many international assets the country owns by looking at change in ownership. The country's budget deficit – the amount it must borrow above its income from taxes to meet the needs of its budget – will also indicate its internal economic health.

In general, what all these things will tell you is how risky the market is at the current moment. An economic decline is a time for safe bets, so it's usually when you'll find traders turning their attention to those safe currencies we discussed. In a time of increase, they will look more towards riskier currencies, which include the Canadian dollar, the Australian dollar, the New Zealand dollar, the British pound and the Euro.

FUNDAMENTAL ANALYSIS

In order to trade in the forex market successfully, one of the most important things you can learn is the most reliable way to spot a trade that is going to end up being reliably profitable from one that blows up in your face. This is where proper analysis comes in handy, whether technical or fundamental. Fundamental analysis is easier to learn, though it is more time consuming to use properly, while technical analysis can be more difficult to wrap your mind around but can be done quite quickly once you get the hang of it. While both will help you to find the information you are looking for, they go about doing so in different ways; fundamental analysis concerns itself with looking at the big picture while technical analysis focuses on the price of a given currency in the moment to the exclusion of all else.

This divide when it comes to information means that fundamental analysis will always be useful when it comes to determining currencies that are currently undervalued based on current market forces. The information that is crucial to fundamental analysis is generated by external sources which means there won't always be new information available at all times. This chapter and the next are dedicated to fundamental and technical analysis, respectively.

Generally speaking, fundamental analysis allows you a likely glimpse at the future of the currency in question based on a variety of different variables such as publicized changes to the monetary policy that the countries you are interested in might affect. The idea here is that with enough information you can then find currency pairs that are currently undervalued because the market hasn't yet had the time to catch up with the changes that have been made. Fundamental analysis is always made up of the same set of steps which are described in detail below.

Start by determining the baseline: When it comes to considering the fundamental aspects of a pair of currencies, the first thing that you are going to want to do is to determine a baseline from which those currencies tend to return to time and again compared to the other commonly traded currency pairs. This will allow you to determine when it is time to make a move as you will be able to easily pinpoint changes to the pair that are important enough to warrant further consideration.

In order to accurately determine the baseline, the first thing you will need to do is to look into any relevant macroeconomic policies that are currently affecting your currency of choice. You will also want to look into the available historical data as past behavior is one of the best indicators of future evets. While this part of the process can certainly prove tedious, their important cannot be overstated.

After you have determined the historical precedent of the currency pair you are curious about, the next thing you will want to consider is the phase the currency is currently in and how likely it is going to remain in that phase for the foreseeable future. Every currency goes through phases on a regular basis as part of the natural market cycle.

The first phase is known as the boom phase which can be easily identified by its low volatility and high liquidity. The opposite of this phase is known as the bust phase wherein volatility is extremely high, and liquidity is extremely low. There are also pre and post versions of both phases that can be used to determine how much time the phase in question has before it is on its way out. Determining the right phase is a key part of knowing when you are on the right track regarding a particular trading pair.

In order to determine the current major or minor phase, the easiest thing to do is to start by checking the current rates of defaults along with banks loans as well as the accumulated reserve levels of the currencies in question. If numbers are relatively low them a boom phase is likely to be on its way, if not already in full swing. If the current numbers have already overstayed their welcome, then you can be fairly confident that a post-boom phase is likely to start at any time. Alternatively, if the numbers in question are higher than the baseline you have already established then you know that the currency in question is either due for a bust phase or is already experiencing it.

You can make money from either of the major phases as long as you are aware of them early on enough to turn a profit before things start to swing back in the opposite direction. Generally speaking, this means that the faster you can pinpoint what the next phase is going to be, the greater your dividends of any related trades will be.

Broaden your scope: After you have a general idea of the baseline for your favored currencies, as well as their current phases, the next thing you will need to do is look at the state of the global market as a whole to determine how it could possibly affect your trading pair. To ensure this part of the process is as effective as possible you are going to need to look beyond the obvious signs that everyone can see to find the indicators that you know will surely make waves as soon as they make it into the public consciousness.

One of the best places to start looking for this information is in the technology sector as emerging technologies can turn entire economies around in a relatively short period of time.

Technological indicators are often a great way to take advantage of a boom phase by getting in on the ground floor as, once it starts, it is likely to continue for as long as it takes for the technology to be fully integrated into the mainstream. Once it reaches the point of complete saturation then a bust phase is likely going to be on the horizon, and sooner rather than later. If you feel as though the countries responsible for the currencies in question are soon going to be in a post-boom or post-bust phase, then you are going to want to be very careful in any speculative market as the drop-off is sure to be coming and it is difficult to pinpoint exactly when.

If you know that a phase shift is coming, but you aren't quite sure when, then it is a good idea to focus on smaller leverage amounts than during other phases as they are more likely to pay off in the short-term. At the same time, you are also going to want to keep any eye out for long-term positions that are likely to pay out if a phase shift does occur. On the other hand, if the phase you are in currently is just starting out, you can make trades that have a higher potential for risk as the time concerns aren't going to be nearly serious enough to warrant the additional caution.

Look to global currency policy: While regional concerns are often going to be able to provide you with an insight into some long-reaching changes a given currency might experience in the near future, you are also going to want to broaden your search, even more, to include relevant global policies as well. While determining where you are going to start can be difficult at first, all you really need to do is to provide the same level of analysis that you used at the micro level on a macro basis instead. The best place to start with this sort of thing is going to be with the interest rates of the major players including the Federal Reserve, the European Central Bank, the Bank of Japan, the Bank of England and any other banks that may affect the currencies you are considering trading.

You will also need to consider any relevant legal mandates or policy biases that are currently in play to make sure that you aren't blindsided by these sorts of things when the times actually comes to stop doing research and actually make a move. While certainly time consuming, understanding every side of all the major issues will make it far easier to determine if certain currencies are flush with supply where the next emerging markets are likely to appear and what worldwide expectations are when it comes to future interest rate changes as well as market volatility.

Don't forget the past: Those who forget the past are doomed to repeat it and that goes double for forex traders. Once you have a solid grasp on the current events of the day, you are going to want to dig deeper and look for scenarios in the past that match what is currently going on today. This level of understanding will ultimately lead to a greater understanding of the current strength of your respective currencies while also giving you an opportunity to accurately determine the length of the current phase as well.

In order to ensure you are able to capitalize on your knowledge as effectively as possible, the ideal time to jump onto a new trade is going to be when one of the currency pairs is entering a post-boom phase while the other is entering the post-bust phase. This will ensure that the traditional credit channels are not exhausted completely, and you will thus have access to the maximum amount of allowable risk of any market state. This level of risk is going to start dropping as soon as the market conditions hit an ideal state and will continue until the situation with the currencies is reversed so getting in and making a profit when the time is right is crucial to your long-term success.

Don't forget volatility: Keeping the current level of volatility in mind is crucial when it comes to ensuring that the investments you are making are actually going to pay off in a reasonable period of time. Luckily, Luckily, it is relatively easy to determine the current level of volatility in a given market, all you need to do is to look to that country's stock market. The greater the level of stability the market in question is experiencing, the more confident those who are investing in it are going to remain when means the more stable the forex market is going to remain as well.

Additionally, it is important to keep in mind that, no matter what the current level of volatility may be, the market is never truly stable. As such, the best traders are those who prepare for the worst while at the same time hoping for the best. Generally speaking, the more robust a boom phase is, the lower the overall level of volatility is going to be.

Think outside the box on currency pairs: All of the information that you gather throughout the process should give you a decent idea regarding the current state of the currency pairs you are keeping tabs on. You should now have enough to be able to use this information to determine which pairs are going to be able to provide you with the most potential profit in not just the short-term but the long-term as well. Specifically, you are going to want to keep an eye out for pairs that have complimentary futures so that they will end up with the greatest gap between their two interest rates as possible.

Additionally, you are going to want to consider the gap between countries when it comes to overall output and unemployment rate. When looking into these differences you are also going to need to be aware of the fact that shortages can cause constraints to capacity or when the unemployment rate drops, both of which can lead to inflation as well. This, in turn, leads to an increase in interest rates which leads to a general cooling of the country's economy. As such, these factors are extremely important when it comes to determining the overall disparity between the interest rates of specific countries in the near future.

Furthermore, you are going to want to keep tabs on the amount of debt that the countries in question are dealing with, as well as their reputation of repayment on the global market. Specifically, you are going to want to look for a balanced capital to debt ratio as the healthier that this number is the stronger the national currency is going to be no matter what else is currently taking place. To determine this ratio, you will want to know how much capital each country currently has on hand as well as their position when it comes to other nations and their level of reserves and foreign investment.

Understand their relative trade strength: If you find a currency that is currently in the middle of a boom phase, the overall strength that its fundamentals show will determine how likely those who are holding it in various currency pairs are to hold or sell. The same also goes for currencies that boast an overly strong or overly weak interest rate when compared to other, similar currencies. What this means is that when a given currency is in the earliest part of the boom phase you will be able to easily find a strong market for its related currency pairs which combine agreeable fundamentals and strong interest rates. While all of these factors are important, as a general rule a strong interest rate will always trump subpar fundamentals.

Watch out for market sentiment

While determining specifics in undervalued currencies is useful most of the time, sometimes the market simply doesn't behave in the way that it realistically should. In these cases, it is the market sentiment that has hijacked the price of the currency in question and learning how to stay on the lookout for its influence is guaranteed to save you from some seriously unprofitable trades in the long run.

Like many things in the forex market, this is easier said than done, however, which is why it is best to take the following suggestions related to reading market sentiment to heart if you ever hope to get a clear idea of how strong the momentum regarding a given currency truly is.

Choose the right trend: Each and every move that a currency makes is ultimately based on a trend that started building hours, if not days before. As such, if you spend time trading with either the 15 or 60-minute chart then you may find yourself accidentally moving forward based on part of a larger trend that is ultimately going to end up moving in the opposite direction. As such, in order to avoid such mistakes, you are going to want to start by identifying the trend in the daily chart and then working inward from there until you reach your target chart. This will allow you to more easily determine the breadth of a given chart and allow you to avoid trading based on anterior movement as well.

Find the right price movement: On the topic of price movement, depending on the pair you are trading in, you will likely come across profits that you might not otherwise bank by simply getting a feel for the way your favored currency pairs move on a regular basis. Getting a feel for price movement means understanding the speed at which the pair typically moves, in both directions, to ensure that you know the most effective time to strike.

When the movement is clearly headed in an upwards direction with a quickness, only to slowly descend after the fact, time and again, then you can expect other traders to be steadily buying into the pair without taking the time to do all the relevant research. This, in turn, means you can expect the overall sentiment of the market to be bullish which means you can respond appropriately.

Similar information can also be determined based on the way the market responds when new relevant information, both positive and negative, comes to light. As an example, if there was just a round of positive economic news out of the United Kingdom but the positive change in the GBP and USD pair doesn't seem all that enthusiastic, then you can safely determine that the market is moving in a bearish direction when it comes to GBP/USD.

Watch your indicators of volume: While there are a wide variety of different indicators that measure volume, there are no better means for doing so than the Commitment of Traders Report which is released each and every Friday. This report clearly outlines the net of all the trades made, both long and short, for the week, for both commercial and private traders. This is a great place to start if you aren't sure what currencies to favor as this will show where most of the interest was for the proceeding week.

As previously noted, it is best to always trade on the trend which means that if there are more net longs overall you are going to want to buy and if there are more net shorts overall then you are going to want to sell. When this is not the case is if the buy positions are already at extreme levels then you will want to sell or at least wait until things move in the other direction because there can be no more increase if everyone who is going to buy has already bought. Eventually, you will see a reversal in this case which means that if this is the case then you are better off trading in the medium term instead.

Look more closely at international trends: When you are first getting your start in the forex market you are likely going to be surprised at just how interconnected the world as a whole really is. While some of these connections are going to be obvious, other will certainly catch you off guard the first time you encounter them which means you will want to pay attention to the way news affects various currency pairs, even if you are not actually trading in them at the moment as you never know when that information might be useful again at a later date.

TECHNICAL ANALYSIS

In order to ensure that your successful trade percentage only continues to increase as time goes on, you will likely eventually find it useful to branch out from using fundamental analysis exclusively to using technical analysis as well. While some traders consider the two types of analysis to be at odds with one another, the fact of the matter is that a balanced approach that uses each, when required, is always going to be the most effective in both the short and the long-term.

Technical analysis studies past market trends with the goal of accurately predicting those that are likely to occur again in the future. Technical analysis is ideal for those that like the idea of determining future performance by looking at previous prices, without having to dig through mountains of paperwork to find the details you are looking for. While the past will never be able to truly predict the future 100 percent of the time, technical analysis is useful when combined with a basic understanding of market mentality for generating predictions that are accurate within reason.

Price charts

A price chart is the primary tool of technical analysis. As the name implies, it charts the price of a given currency, on the x axis, as time passes, on the y axis. There are several different types of charts to choose from, but if you are just getting started with technical analysis then you will want to start with the line chart, the point and click chart, the candlestick chart and the bar chart.

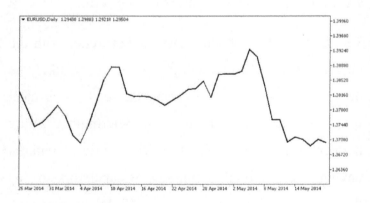

Line charts: The most basic chart of them all is the line chart. It shows the closing price for the currency in question over a set period of time. The titular line is then formed one the day's grouping of closing prices has been determined and they are then connected with the purpose of determining a trend. While it doesn't include relevant details such as opening price or the results for the day overall, it will tell you if the day is positive or negative while also cutting out all of the noise that is so common in most other charts. As such, it can be an extremely enlightening place to start if you are looking at a new currency for the first time.

Bar chart: When compared to a line chart, a bar chart adds in the additional details related to a currency's movement throughout each day. The top and the bottom of the bar are going to represent the high and low for the day respectively and the closing price is denoted by a dash found on the right side of the bar. Meanwhile, the dash on the left side of the bar is going to show the starting price. Finally, if the overall value of the currency increased for the day then the bar will be black and if it decreased it will be either red or clear depending on your trading software.

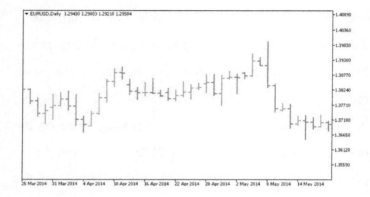

Candlestick chart: A candlestick is similar to a bar chart in many ways, though it also provides additional relevant information that is more detailed overall. It includes the range for the day, expressed as a line, as with a bar graph, but when you view a candlestick chart you will also notice a wide bar near the vertical line which indicates the degree of difference the price experienced over a given period of time. If the price increases for the day, then the candlestick will not be shaded in and if the price decreased throughout the day then it will typically be shaded in red as well.

Point and figure chart: While the point and figure chart are used less frequently than some of the charts that have been previously discussed, the point and figure chart has been in constant use for more than 100 years and can still provide insight when used correctly. Specifically, this chart is used to determine how much a price is likely to move without taking timing or volume into account. This makes it a pure indicator of price, without any of the market noise that might otherwise be attached.

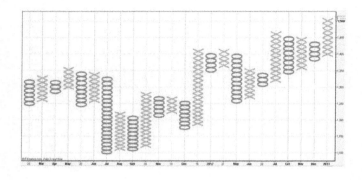

A point and figure chart can be easily picked out from the crowd as it is made up of Xs and Os rather than lines and points. The Xs will indicate points where positive trends occurred while the Os will indicate periods of downward movement. You will also notice numbers and letters listed along the bottom of the chart which corresponds to months as well as dates. This type of chart will also make it clear how much the price is going to have to move in order for an X to become an O or an O to become an X.

Range and trend

In order to ensure that you can properly profit from the use of technical analysis, it is crucial that you determine if it makes more sense for your trading style to focus on trading via trend or trading via range. While the two are both based on the price of the currency in question, they use that information quite differently in practice which means you are going to want to focus on either one or the other for the best results.

If you feel as though your personal trading style would benefit from making trades that mostly go with the flow, then you are going to be more interested in trading via trend as this will tell you what other traders are up to. Your goal in situations like this will be to determine which trends are most likely going to be the most robust in the near future, so you have the maximum amount of time to jump on them, reaping a lion's share of the profits in the process. If you are considering this type of trading, then you will want to stick with smaller trades as you can lose out if a trend fails to materialize in the expected way at the wrong time. Trading via trend is ideal for those who prefer high risk and the greater potential for reward it brings along with it.

Range trading, on the other hand, is better suited for those who are willing to forgo some amount of profit for more reliable returns. The range in question is going to be the price that a given currency is going to return to twice or more throughout the time you are holding it, allowing you to profit each time. The market is going to present you with different challenges every single day in the form of different trends and potential opportunities.

Regardless of this fact, the movement typically tends to operate in ways that seem completely random, though its true intentions can be found once you determine where to look. The opening range has been profitable for trading professionals for decades as a profitable way to start off with an idea of the market's mood to make any profits that are coming up even easier to obtain.

When you take advantage of the opening range for a starting point, you ill then be able to locate the truth of the current market to determine if the bulls or bears are going to be in charge at the moment. In order to get the most out of this practice, it is crucial that you understand the opening range for low and high levels as they are of critical importance when it comes to levels of resistance and support throughout the day.

Understanding these details will make it far easier for you to anticipate levels in the market that are more likely to reverse or increase the changes you are seeing. Looking at the trading day from this perspective is going to make it easier for you to make the right moves at the right time to allow you to determine when future movement is forthcoming, so you can be in the right place at the right time.

This doesn't mean you won't be able to act if you can't find the perfect entry point each and every time. All it means is that you will simply need to get in at a point where you will be in an ideal position for the next time the cycle repeats itself. You should also keep in mind that of the two strategies, range trading can take more resources to utilize properly which means you will want to have a substantial bankroll before you put it into effect.

Start off on the right foot

In order to use technical analysis effectively, you will need to understand that it functions around the idea that the price of a given currency is going to fluctuate in the future based on a number of identifiable patterns that can be seen in its past. As such, unlike with fundamental analysis where you might have trouble finding enough data to make a rational choice, with technical analysis you will have more data than you can ever hope to sort through. You will have plenty of tools to help you sort through all of this information, including things like trends, charts and indicators that will point you in the right direction.

While many of the technical analysis techniques might seem overly complicated at first, at their most basic they are all looking for different ways to determine trends that are going to form in the future along with the strength. Choosing the right trends at the right time is the first step to becoming a successful forex trader in the long-term.

Understand the market: Technical analysis is all about measuring the relative value of a particular trade or underlying asset by using available tools to find otherwise invisible patterns that, ideally, few other people have currently noticed. When it comes to using technical analysis properly you are going to always need to assume three things are true. First and foremost, the market ultimately discounts everything; second, trends will always be an adequate predictor of price and third, history is bound to repeat itself when given enough time to do so.

Technical analysis also believes that the price of a given underlying asset is ultimately the only metric that truly matters when it comes to understanding the current state of the market. This is the case because any and all other facets of the market have already been factored through to the price before it reached the point it is currently at which means that analyzing anything besides the price is, simply put, a waste of time.

Furthermore, technical analysis holds to the fact that the value of the underlying asset in question moves based on a trend that is well established which means it can be tracked as long as you know what it is that you are looking for. From there, it is really just a matter of time before the trend comes back around and you can take advantage of it once more. This is a viable strategy as it is more likely that an existing trend is going to reemerge than it is for a completely new trend to show up in its place.

After all, history is always going to repeat itself. This isn't just a saying, it is an unavoidable part of human nature, specifically, people like patterns. This means that if there is a pattern in a series of data, you can expect people to find it. Once it is found, you can then rest assured that they will do everything they can to take advantage of it. This will be the case each and every time the pattern is found which means that, if you find the pattern first, you can set yourself up to take advantage of it in the most effective way possible.

This is what allows many of the common technical patterns that are in use today to continue to be useful despite the fact that they have been in use for 100 years or more. This just goes to show that public opinion and action in relation to price changes is always going to be the same no matter what.

All about trend: Being aware of trend and how it can affect the ways you will analyze a specific trade is key to your long-term success through technical analysis. When on the lookout for trend, it can be any clear direction that the price of a given currency is taking that is clear enough to cut through all of the noise that naturally infects the market as a whole. Trends can be either strong enough to see from a mile away or weak enough to easily miss even if you are looking for them. Essentially it just means that just because a given trend isn't immediately visible then this doesn't mean it isn't there. Likewise, you are going to always want to ensure that the trend you think you are following is really there as it can be easy to misinterpret false data if you aren't careful.

The best way to ensure that the trend you are following is actually worth following is going to be to focus exclusively on the lows and highs and leave everything else out of the equation. This way you will be able to easily determine if the lows continue to increase (signaling an uptrend) or if the highs continue to decrease (signaling a reversal). You may also uncover a horizontal trend which shows that nothing much of anything is happening at the moment and you might be better off waiting to get into the market until something more well-defined comes along.

Tapping into a specific long-lasting trend can allow you to assume that the net time it comes back around it is likely to be even more pronounced. You will want to keep an eye on things until the trend starts to materialize, however, just in case. If you find yourself watching a short trend, then you will need to expand your focus and ensure you aren't looking at a smaller part of a larger trend by mistake. The easiest way to do so is to simply choose a longer timeframe and see what there is to see.

While this will naturally make things more cumbersome, it can also make it far easier to catch a mistake that you may not otherwise be aware that you are making. The opposite can be true as well, if you are having trouble catching the right shorter trend, then a narrow focus across a shorter timeline might be just what the doctor ordered.

Trend mapping: After you have picked out the trend you are interested in finding more about, the next thing you will need to do is create a trendline that will let you map out all of the details as you come across them. This can be accomplished by simply drawing a straight line through the data points to make the trend more visible. If the trend is positive, then you will want to connect the dots of the various lows that are being measured while if it is a negative trend you will want to connect the relevant highs.

This line is what is known as the resistance line and it represents the market's natural inclination to push back once prices hit a point that is either significantly above or significantly below the average. This doesn't indicate the likelihood of the next price movement, just its overall limits. Once you have created the initial line, you will then want to create an additional pair of lines, one for the support level and one for the resistance level.

The support line will connect all of the lows while the resistance lines will connect all of the highs. The resulting channel that you then create will likely be either positive or negative though neutral channels representing sideways movement are also possible. Regardless, the channel you create needs to continue for a long enough time to show where the price breaks away from the status quo. This moment is going to represent your ideal entry point that will give you the best chance see the greatest overall return on your investment.

CURRENCY FORECASTING - WHAT BOOKWORMS ECONOMISTS LOOK AT

For many beginner traders, the most complicated part that comes with this type of trading is how to understand the way currency trading actually takes place and how to get into the market well. The common mistake here is to make the assumption that it is a simple form of trading because it's top level. You are not dealing with what money can buy because you are dealing with the money itself. However, the market isn't really going to work with individual currencies as many people think.

Instead, the market can work with currency pairs. While there are about 180 currencies throughout the world, there are thousands of different ways that you can pair them. And the way that you pair them can make a big difference as well because dealing with GBP/USD can be different from doing USD/GBP. Along with the pairings, you have to worry about the meaning that is associated with the order you choose. It does really matter which of the currencies is listed first in the pair and which one goes second.

The first currency is going to be considered the base currency. This is going to represent a total of one, and it is going to be the stable base on which all the trade is going to be founded on. The base currency is going to answer the question "One of these equals X amount of that." So, if you are doing USD/GBP, you would leave the USD as 1, and then fill in the GBP based on that information.

The second currency that is listed there is going to be the quote currency. This is the one that will change to reflect what the relationship between the two currencies in the pair is. The higher it is, the more of the second currency you are going to get when you trade it with the base currency. For example, if one GBP equals 1.4 USD, then for every British pound you decide to trade, you will end up with $1.40 in American dollars.

This is where the jargon can sometimes get a bit confusing to the beginner. When you are ready to trade in Forex, you are either going to do a bid or an offer/ask. The difference between these is below:

- To bid, you are going to sell the base currency, the one on the left of the pairing, for the quote currency that is on the right-hand side of the pair. You will basically buy the base currency and then sell the quote currency.
- To offer or ask, you are going to buy the base currency on the left of the pair in exchange for selling the quote currency in the right-hand side of the pair.

It is important to know the differences between these two because the income that you can make on this trade is going to depend on the relationship that occurs with the two currencies. Get it the wrong way around, and you will end up making a loss, even if you thought that you would make a profit.

It is also important to know that the Forex market is going to deal with how the values of these two chosen currencies are changing. If the value of one increase, it doesn't always mean that the other value is decreasing. Though these two are going to be paired together in the trade, they are not solely going to be influenced by each other. You are just taking two cogs out of a big machine and then comparing them at that particular moment in time.

The speed that the two currencies will change is not always an easy thing to match either. Just because the USD is increasing quickly doesn't mean that the Canadian dollar will increase at the same rate, even if it is increasing. This is where some understanding of the currency market can be useful. Just looking at the pairing isn't going to let you know much about how it's going to look when the market closes or anything else. You need to take a look at the overall trend of the individual currencies and how they have been doing over time, as well as the news events in a particular country, to help you figure this out.

Of course, the clearest trades are going to be the ones that happen when one currency becomes weak against the other. This allows you to purchase or sell the weak currency at a great price. However, it is possible for you to still make a nice profit even when both of them are strengthening, as long as they do this at a different speed. We will spend more time recognizing these signs and understanding how this can profit you later in this guidebook.

How to Choose Your Currency Pairs

Picking out the currency pairs that you want to work with can be very important. While there are a lot of different currencies out there, the market is often dominated by eight main currencies. These can include the American Dollar, the British Pound, the Euro, the Japanese yen, the Australian dollar, the New Zealand Dollar, and the Canadian Dollar.

The first of the pairs are going to be known as the major pairs, and they are the ones that are the most heavily traded in the Forex market. They are also the ones that tend to get the most focus overall compared to the others. Many people find that they are the most comfortable trading in their own currency when they first get started. You can have complete control over this though to make it work for you.

Let's take a little closer look at some of the most important currencies on the market and the roles that they are going to play in the Forex market.

- **The USD:** This is the top currency in the Forex market. America has one of the largest economies in the world, and it is seen as pretty safe to invest in because of this fact. The USD is backed by the Federal reserve and commodities, like energy products and gold are priced in USD. You will notice that many traders go back to the dollar when there are any times of uncertainty because it is one of the safest places to store money. As a new trader, this is a safe and lower risk place to start investing your money.

- **Euro:** This is a currency that covers a lot of Europe, so it is definitely one to watch out for. It's sometimes seen as a bit more unstable because it has to rely on the economies of several different countries at the same time. Things like the Brexit vote have made the value of this currency change the volatility and value and some of the effects of what one country does can be unexpected and strange.

- **The British pound:** Britain decided not to join with using the Euro when it joined the European Union and kept with the pound. Except in times where there is a lot of turmoil, this currency tends to stay stable and steady. And since London is the financial capital of the world, this currency is often seen as safe.

- **Japanese yen:** This is another safe currency for traders to look into and it is where a lot of focus goes when there are times of uncertainty. The Bank of Japan is also one that will step in more than other national banks if there is a concern about how strong the yen is growing and if it will affect the industries of that country. Its overall objective here is to protect the market, and it will do what is necessary to do this.

- **The Swiss franc:** The Swiss central bank has no problem coming in and intervening in the market if it is needed. Switzerland is known as the world's safest place to bank, and much of its economy is invested in the gold prices since the bank holds huge amounts of this metal in reserves to keep the franc stable.

- **The Australian dollar:** This is a currency that is going to be dependent on the commodities market because the country relies on energy resources and mining. The price of gold can impact this currency strongly. Australia trades a lot with China, so if there is a change in the economy of one, there will be in another. The Australian economy is often known for its strength and its ability to rebound after any economic crises, so this can still be a safe option to go with, even with some of the volatility that comes with the commodities market.

- **The New Zealand dollar:** New Zealand is known as an exporter of goods including food products. This is a stable currency because the economy of this country is often good.

- **The Canadian Dollar:** This is going to be another currency that relies on commodities such as oil. Oil is the bedrock of the economy in Canada, and it often trades with the U.S. This means that the two economies will be reliant on each other a little bit. Any events or news that concern oil will have some effects on both economies and the value of their currencies.

Picking from the choices above can make a world of difference when it comes to helping you see results. You will be able to rely on a currency that is relatively safe and won't end up falling while you hold onto it. There are many other currency pairs that you can choose from, but not all of them are as safe to work with, and the volatility of them and their market can make a big difference in how much you are actually able to make with your investment.

When you look at the major currency pairs, then you might notice that they have the US dollar on one side of the pair. The three-letter codes for the currencies are set by the International Standardization Organization (ISO). The following table helps you understand the various names given to the most frequently traded currency pairs.

Currency Pair	Trade Name	Nickname
EUR/USD	Euro-dollar	No nickname
USD/JPY	Dollar-yen	No nickname
GBP/USD	Sterling-dollar	Sterling or Cable
USD/CHF	Dollar-Swiss	Swissy
USD/CAD	Dollar-Canada	Loonie
AUD/USD	Australian-dollar	Aussie or Oz
NZD/USD	New Zealand-dollar	Kiwi

Chapter 3: THE NEED TO BE OBJECTIVE

You might make mistakes in the beginning. That is okay. Just make sure that you are not taking big risks, or you might end up making some rather costly mistakes.

Here are a few steps to help you become a professional trader.

Practice Makes Perfect

There is no easier way around it. There are no shortcuts to becoming a master of the trade game. You have to put in the effort and research to gain the experience and knowledge to handle the markets fluidly. On many trading platforms, you can also make use of demo trading. This form of trading allows you to work on your skills without using real money. They provide you with a particular virtual amount that you can use to perform your trades.

Procrastination Means Missing Out on the Action

Do not leave something for the next day if you can do it today. The forex market does not wait for your decisions. It is an ever-shifting world where changes occur every minute. The trend that you noticed today may not be available to you tomorrow, which is why always keep your goals in sight and your stop-losses firmly established. Focus on what changes you would like to implement.

Monitoring a Profit Objective

Once you have set an objective, let the trade work out. Do not panic at every single turn or during every shift in the currency value. Exit the trade when you have reached your profit objective for the day or if the trade reaches your stop-loss.

Keep on Learning

Do not hesitate to admit that you have made a mistake. The most important thing to note is that you can recover and become a better trader if you are willing to admit that your plan did not go well. Gather more information from other traders or from your own research. See what you can do better. Learn to improve your techniques.

Know Your Capabilities

One of the most important tips that I can recommend for a beginner trader is to begin using small amounts. Do not invest everything you have, no matter how profitable you think a trade might be. Then you can gradually begin to increase the value of your investment with the profit that you earn. Remember that the profit that you earn does not depend on the amount you have invested, which is why you should learn to maximize your profit, however small it is. By opening with small amounts, you minimize the risk of massive losses that occur that large amounts of money bring you. This is a vital component to understand how forex functions and how to trade in the markets.

Currency Pair

Start out with a single currency pair. By now, we know that the world of currency trading is complicated because of the unpredictable situations of global economies. It is not easy to be perfect in the forex market. In fact, it is almost impossible to remain perfect. Which is why I would advise you to start your forex journey by focusing on a single currency pair. Pick a pair that you are confident about or familiar with. Also, think about those pairs that can provide you with sufficient information or the right kind of information. For example, you can choose to use the currency of your country. This is because you may be equipped to understand the economic and political situations of your country. This will make it easier for you to practice your skills in the forex market.

STEP-BY-STEP SECRETS TO WIN WITH FOREX

We just stepped into the emotional world of forex trading. Let us examine some psychological factors that you need to consider while making a trade.

Overcoming Fear

When you as a trader receive some negative news or information about a certain trade in the forex market, it's not strange to get worried or, in some cases, even scared. You might have the tendency to overreact, especially if you are new to the market. You might feel obliged to cut short your losses and get your money back. After all, it's better to cash out right now than face any more risks in the future. However, if you do that, then you may sidestep some losses, but you may also be walking away from some gains.

You need to realize what fear is. Fear is a natural response to what you recognize as a threat—in this case, to your profit or the potential to make more money. Measuring that fear might help as it is only through awareness that you can slowly begin to chip away the negative feeling. You should also try to reflect on what raises the fear in you.

By contemplating the problem of fear ahead of time and understanding how you may unconsciously respond to or recognize certain things (for example, how do you react to dips in the currency value), you can hope to separate and identify those feelings during a trade. When you are able to identify the feelings, you can easily counter them. You can attempt to use your efforts to move past the emotional situation you are facing.

As with all emotions, this ability to learn about your fear is not easy. It may take practice, but it is necessary to be able to know about yourself because the status of your trading portfolio depends on it.

Overcoming Greed

"Pigs get slaughtered" is a pretty popular saying in Wall Street. What does this mean? This saying mentions greedy investors or traders holding on to winning trades or stocks for too long, hoping to get every last benefit they can get out of it. In the world of forex trading, greed can be one of your biggest downfalls. The inability to accurately predict where the market is going can sometimes mean that the value of your trade can take a sudden nosedive.

That means everything you have achieved so far does not matter.

You have lost it all.

Greed can be destructive to returns because you may end up running the risk of getting thrown out of a profitable position quicker than you can react.

Unfortunately, greed is not easy to fall out of. The feeling of greed is dependent on the instinct to keep going just to try to gain just a little more. Do not let greed overwhelm you. You should learn to recognize your impulses and develop a trading strategy that has rational decisions as its foundation. Your instincts cannot dictate the way the market goes. Your keen knowledge, attention, and experience can.

Establish Rules

In order to prepare yourself for a trade, try to start from a clear frame of mind before you feel the psychological effects. The way you can do this is by creating clear and set rules for yourself. You should put down guidelines based on your tolerance to handle risk and reward. This will allow you to find out where you would like to enter a trade and when you would like to exit it. You can choose to create a profit target method where you aim for a specific profit goal based on realistic expectations and current market information, or you can choose to use a stop-loss method where you stop a trade regardless of how it proceeds so that you can cut losses early, should they appear.

You should also consider establishing certain limits on the amount you are willing to win or lose every day. If you are able to reach a profit target, they take the money and think no more of it. If you are losing on your trades and your losses reach a predetermined limit that is set by you, then stop what you are doing and cut short your losses.

You can always return and have another go at the market, but you can never return from a massive blow to your finances. In fact, you might find yourself in a terrible situation that might affect your life and your future.

Do not go there. Make sure you are careful and thoughtful about your trades.

Research

There is no replacement for good information. If you are making trades because of guesses, then stop immediately! You should aim to learn as much as you can about your particular trade and the forex market in general. Educate yourself and, if possible, attend various trade seminars and conferences. You should be hungry for more information.

Additionally, while we have broached the subject of research, you need to set aside a time every day to know more about global events, currency fluctuations, economic and political conditions, and every other factor that could affect your trade. You should also devote time to study charts, communicate with other traders (if possible), or even read trade magazines and publications. This helps you remain aware of the trade and the market.

DANGERS OF GETTING EMOTIONAL ABOUT FOREX TRADE

You are the person behind the trades, and your emotional and psychological well-being is important to make sure that you are reacting to the forex market properly.

Let us talk about the psychology of trading and some ways to make yourself a better trader.

We are going to dabble in a bit of psychology (as if that wasn't obvious from the title). Here, we are going to focus solely on your emotions—not in relation to a trade but in relation to yourself.

If you find your emotions spiraling out of control, then try the following techniques.

Figure Out What You Are Feeling

When you are enduring a surge of negative emotions, take a time out and ask yourself what you are really feeling right now.

Is it anger that you feel? Or is your anger a mask to hide something else?

You Are the Master

You do not serve your emotions. Your emotions serve you.

Taking the time to understand your problem helps you master your emotions and prevent you from reacting in the same manner in the future.

Here are some questions that you can ask yourself when you feel that your emotions are leading you astray:

- What can I learn from my emotions? Why did I react that way?
- How would I really like to feel?
- What should I focus on to be in a state where I am the master of my emotions?
- What steps can I take right now?

There Is a Way

Know that using your emotions as a tool only serves to land you in a terrible situation. You need to realize that you have to keep a rational mind. If the trade is benefiting you, then make sure that you do not react too positively. Try to be analytical so that you do not end up making a mistake where you take bigger and bigger risks just because you are having a spell of good fortune.

If the trade does not go well, do not panic. Firstly, check your stats and the news. Find out more about your trade. If the result is truly bad, then find out what you can do about it.

By simply taking the time out to focus on your emotions, you are dealing with one problem at a time. It is not easy (and frankly not recommended) to split your mind between the trades and your present frame of mind. You need to be able to keep your focus clear to deal with the uncertainties that are definitely going to arise in the future.

Chapter 4: FOREX TRADING STRATEGY

When choosing a Forex strategy, you may not just have to factor-in the success profit and rate portion. You would likewise require considering carefully your lifestyle and just what system enables you to fit or suit it. You'll need to know just what Forex system that is trading be utilized appropriately in your time zone.

A method that is beneficial in foreign exchange trading is what is called leverage. The total amount of the money that you will be trading in your account with the leverage strategy, you would earn about one hundred times. Plenty of traders have testified that they were able to win a whole great deal of profit by using this sort of strategy. To help you make use of this strategy to have more benefits if you have a funded Forex account.

Automated currency trading is kind that is another system or strategy. Entering and exiting an order shall be determined by your automatic system. Again, the price and the real point where the program would come or exit a trade is predetermined.

CHANNEL BREAKOUT

These are the trends that will break out of the resistance and support curve, and often, they show up after a new event, or a piece of news is released. This is where you will want to bring in your knowledge of the economy so that you can determine when a breakout is going to occur. If you guess correctly, you can get into the market before the price goes up and sell when it reaches its top. Or you can get out of the market in time if the news is bad or brings up uncertainty before the market crashes and you lose out on all your money.

Many traders find that working with a technical analysis can be a great option to help them earn a good amount of money on the Forex market. It does require looking at a lot of charts and graphs to see success. But for those who can learn about the trends that occur with a specific currency, and who are willing to watch out for some big news items that may change the course of their currency pair away from its historical values, then a technical analysis may be the right option for you.

THE IMPORTANCE OF REAL POWER STRATEGY

It is a 24-Hours market

You might have come across many markets in the financial industry. But, have you come across a market that is accessible 24-hours a day? But, if you consider the Forex market, you will be able to trade anytime you want because it is open for 24-hours. This is a worldwide market, so it is obvious why it will be open. The market gives access in on a Sunday in Australia and closes on Friday in New York. Thus, the Forex market doesn't cease, so traders are always welcome to trade the market. If you are willing to trade part-time, this is a great opportunity for you because you will be able to trade any time you want.

A highly liquid market

By now, you would have figured out the term liquidity. Anyway, liquidity means how quick an asset can be turned into cash. So, when you look at the Forex market, you will understand that it is highly liquid. Also, this is a great benefit because you can easily enter into trades and make money with a few clicks. As someone from the other end of the market will be looking forward to trade, you'll never run out of chances. Like mentioned earlier, if you don't like manual trade setup, you can set limit order or stop-loss to react automatically. However, this highly liquid market will benefit you immensely.

The costs are lower

Unlike other markets, you don't have to bear a lot of costs because costs are lower in Forex trading. The major cost that you will deal in Forex trading is spread. However, the spread is not a huge cost when compared to other markets' costs in the industry. But, remember, when you use a long-term trading strategy, you might have to bear swap cost as well. However, the costs related to Forex trading is lower.

The Leverage

You have already come across leverage. Anyway, it is better to understand the benefit of leverage. As beginners, you must get a clear view of every important factor in the market. So, leverage is offered by brokers, so that gives you the opportunity to trade above your deposit. Basically, you'll be able to control larger trades even if you have a smaller amount in your account. With the help of leverage, you will be able to make more profits and keep risks under control. Even though leverage looks like a great benefit, it is actually risky at a certain point. If you don't utilize risk management concept, you will end up overleveraging and losing your account. Thus, you must make sure to handle leverage carefully and correctly. It will not take long for a benefit to turn into a loss.

Profit potential

When you consider currency trading, you must see the apparent benefits in it. For example, even if the value of a currency pair increase or decreases, you are benefitted if you trade vigilantly. You can consider the options to go long or go short as per the market movement. Hence, this market has profit potential. As a beginner, you must remember to focus on the learning process if you want to enjoy this potential profit benefit. Most naïve traders enter into the market and gamble because they don't know how to trade Forex. But, if you want to become successful, you must make an effort to understand the market.

No fixed position size or commissions

The best things about the Forex market are immense. However, I have shortlisted a few. So, if you are in the Forex market, you get to decide the position size which is not possible in the futures market. Hence, you can start trading even with a small trading account. Also, Forex trading doesn't involve an exchange fee, clearing fee, brokerage fee, or government fee. But, you must bear the spread cost that is paid to the Forex traders for obtaining their service.

A decentralized market

As you are aware, the Forex market is a massive market, and nobody can control it. Each day a large number of participants enter the market so not a single entity can control it. Thus, the Forex market is a decentralized market that cannot be controlled by anyone. So, eventually, you become your boss when you trade Forex.

Easy entry

If you want to enter the Forex market, you can do it. You don't need a huge capital and many qualifications to enter into Forex trading. When you compare other markets in the financial industry, you will not find any other markets that accept lower capital. However, when you are opening an account with an online broker, you might have met their minimum deposit amount, and roughly, it is as little as $25. But, I'm not recommending to open a trading account with $25. Instead, I'm explaining the easy entry that Forex offers to its traders. Due to this factor, the Forex market has become an accessible market.

Free demo account

Almost all the Forex brokers provide demo trading opportunity when you sign up with them. Actually, this demo trading account option is a great tool for newcomers as well as professionals. For beginners, the demo account is like a practice account. They can use it to test new strategies, techniques, and skills. In fact, you don't have to trade the real trading account when you are trading for the first time. Instead, you can trade the demo account because it will not cost money and you can practice as much as you want. On the other hand, professional traders can try newly developed techniques and methods on the demo account before trying them out on the live account so that they don't have to lose their hard-earned money.

Complete control

Well, you have control over the things that you do. Nobody can force you to take up a trade or to leave a trade because the decision is solely yours. You will not find a single person controlling you which is freedom. Thus, when you are trading Forex as a full-time career, you get to enjoy the privilege of being your own boss. But remember, when you are deciding to trade full-time ensure that you have completely understood the market. Also, make sure to save some money, so if full-time trading doesn't work, you have a backup plan. But, full-time trading has worked for many. So, if you want it to work for you, it is important to have a defined, long-term plan.

Market transparency

The large Forex market doesn't hide its information, and rather it is transparent. The general public can access the information to make a trading decision. But remember, the transparency of the Forex market isn't easy to understand. Thus you must do your homework. You must make an effort to understand the market information because it is not easy to interpret.

THE ADVANTAGES OF AUTOMATED FOREX TRADING

There are ways to understand in case your currency trading strategy is excellent or successful.

- Start knowing how effective it has been in the past. It will pay to learn simply how much previous or current users associated with the operational system have received so far by utilizing the strategy. Regardless of that, additionally obtain some informative data on how much is the drawdown that is maximum of system in its previous trading.

- There was a win-loss ratio which it is possible to check. It is about how much you have won compared with much you have actually lost. Apart from that, there is also a profit-loss ratio. This s about the average winning trade set alongside the trade that is losing.

- You would also need to know how consistent the system is in delivering earnings.

CALCULATING INTEREST ON FOREX TRADES

This is going to involve liberal use of math, so you should be prepared. Actually, here is the perfect moment to add in a little advice. If you are not comfortable with pips and lots, then don't jump in on a trade. Try to familiarize yourself with these terms and the way they work. This is because when you finally start trading, you should be aware of the changes happening to the currency on every level. With that small recommendation, let us move on.

I am going to use the fourth decimal point system for the example below. If you can understand it, then you can apply the same calculation to a five-decimal-point system as well.

We have now established that EUR/USD shifted from 1.1183 to 1.1184. Therefore, currently, EUR/USD = 1.1184 or in other words, 1 EUR to 1.1184 USD. We represent this as 1 EUR/1.1184 USD.

We simply have to replace the above components with values.

We know for certain the following: The amount of change in the value of the counter currency is 0.0001 USD. The rate of exchange is 1 EUR/1.1184 USD.

In the end, we are looking at the following value:

[0.0001 USD] × [1 EUR/1.1184 USD]

We can shift the values around so that the equation looks like the following:

[0.0001 USD/1.1184 USD] × 1 EUR

This gives us the following value:

0.00008941344 EUR

The above value of the euro is what you get for every one unit that you trade.

Now let us assume that you have chosen to pick up a mini-lot of 10,000 units of the EUR/USD. When there is a single change of pip in the exchange rate of the currencies, then the entire change in the value would be 10,000 units × 0.00008941344 EUR. This would give us roughly 0.89 EUR change in the position of the value of the currency exchange.

Of course, the keyword to remember is "roughly" as every time the exchange rate shifts, so does the value of each pip.

The above example is just a simple explanation of the way pips work. When you are working with the forex market, you might have to make a note of the values in order to make the best trade.

Chapter 5: FOREX TRADING PSYCHOLOGY

Psychology and trading, most people might think that these factors don't relate to one another. Well, it very well does. As I mentioned earlier, most trading mistakes occur because the traders don't understand the importance of trading psychology. However, most traders don't trade successfully, mainly because of emotional problems. Especially, naïve traders don't handle emotions well, so they don't remain in the market for long. But, it is not something good which is why educating naïve traders is important. Even before they enter the market, it is important to spend the time to learn the market. However, the most common issue with trading is fear. But, fear is commonly seen when the trader moves into the live trading account. But, initially, the temptation is often found in naïve traders. When they enter the market, they enter with the thought of trading as much as possible to make money. Hence, this thought will not let them achieve what they actually should achieve. Therefore, when a trader is tempted to trade, he or she may trade even without analyzing or anticipating the trades.

However, as mentioned fear can also create a lot of issues in a trader's journey. Many traders give up trading completely because of fear. But, the fight or flight reaction is a human thing, that is commonly seen in traders. But actually, this reaction cannot be changed that easily, but of course, traders can handle this reaction wisely. If you study trading psychology, things will become simpler when trading the Forex market. Anyway, when you fear to trade, it will impact your trading behaviors negatively. Most of the time, you will look for a safer method to trade and, perhaps, it is not possible to find safer trading methods in the Forex market.

As you already know, the Forex market involves a lot of risks, so as traders, you must learn to handle them carefully. For example, when you enter into a trade, your instincts point out the chances of losing and you will eventually exit from the trade, and it might have been a profitable trade. So see, your mind has a direct connection to the way you trade.

Even if you have a defined plan, you can still steer away from trading because the power of psychology is immense. You might even become anxious and consider short-term positions because you are afraid to enter into long-term positions even if they seem profitable. Well, yes, fear, greed, and all the other emotions can cause a lot of problems to your trading journey. Hence, you must understand trading psychology. If you do, you will be able to assist those emotions wisely and handle trading successfully. Normally, if you overcome fear, it will be beneficial to your trading journey as well as life.

Typically, traders don't fear the market when they are preparing to enter into a trade, but when the market opens, their emotions play the role. As humans, you can never get rid of emotions because it is a part of humankind. But, you can always learn the methods to control your emotions when excitement is a dangerous emotion when trading the Forex market. When you are excited, you might make mistakes when entering a trade or anticipating market movements. Thus, when you are trading, you have to try to keep your emotions neutral.

Most traders succumb to accept that they are making trading mistakes that are related to psychology. But normally, when people can't accept, denial is the first reaction. Over time, they tend to accept the truth. Just like that, even the naïve traders will learn to accept the truth. However, Forex trading is not only about trading system and strategies. You must accept that mindset is an important part of Forex trading. The way you anticipate the Forex market has a lot to do with trading. Also, only if you understand the trades will you be able to enter into it. Thus, a trader's mindset has a lot to do with trading.

If you look at certain websites that advertise robotic trading systems, you might find trading psychology as an absurd thing. But, remember, those trading systems will not provide benefits as they portray. Nothing is as best as trading manually. You must use your knowledge and skills to trade the market; only then will you be able to trade successfully. Also, those websites are doing their duty to market their product, and if you rely on them and purchase it, you might have to pay them for using their product. Hence, when you come across something like this, make sure to think logically. As a beginner, you must try to settle for a simple yet effective strategy, so that you will be able to trade peacefully.

Anyway, why do you think most naïve traders struggle to make money? You might have seen many people who fail in trading the Forex market. Well, there are many reasons why traders fail, but the major reason is the ones who enter the Forex market don't really know the market. A higher percentage of traders enter into the Forex market by believing the fabricated ads. And it makes them set unrealistic goals. Eventually, they struggle to meet those unrealistic goals and end up quitting trading. But the worst part is that there are traders who quit their day job after they enter the Forex market. Well, it is not a wise move because they must test to check whether trading works for them. Or some other traders believe trading is easy money and no matter how many times I repeat it, some people still believe it is possible. These thoughts create tension and stress, so eventually, the trader becomes emotionally unstable. Thus, when traders trade with an emotionally unstable mindset, they lose money.

PSYCHOLOGY OF A SUCCESSFUL TRADER IN THE FOREX MARKET

So, how can a trader develop a trading mindset? If you want to develop a trading mindset, you need to do your part. It is important to put the required effort to accomplish what you are looking for. Well, you can't build a trading mindset that quickly because you have to learn and accept the Forex market as it is. If you try to deny facts about the Forex market, you will not be able to create a trading mindset.

You must start developing your trading mindset by handling the risks in trading. First of all, understand that risk management isn't for one trade, preferably it is applicable for all the trades that you enter into. You must make sure to calculate the risk for each trade before you enter into it. When you are managing risks, certain emotions might try to confuse you, but you must not let it happen. Once you start handling your emotions wisely, you will be able to manage trades also. However, the simplest way to control emotion when managing risks is to risk ONLY the amount that you can lose. You must create a mindset that enters into a trade while knowing the probability of losing trade. If you follow this, you will be able to remain in the trading world for a long time. But, it takes practice and patience to create a trading mindset that accepts losses. Also, you must master your trading edge. No matter what trading strategy you are using, you must know it completely to trade successfully.

And, remember, overtrading will never create profits. Instead, overtrading will blow all your hard-earned money. You must trade only when you actually see a profit signal. Don't try to trade just because you feel like trading. Or don't try to guess trade because that doesn't work in Forex trading. If you overtrade, it can be challenging to stop, and you'll become an emotional trader.

If you want to build a trading mindset, you must have an organized mindset. So, basically, when you have an organized mindset, you will think about the trading plan, journal, and much more. You must accept the fact that Forex trading is a business. Hence, don't try to gamble in the market. When you are making trading decisions, you must remain calm and steady; only then will you be able to think clearly.

But then, after you build a trading mindset, you must not let emotions play their role. However, the most common emotions that you must avoid are:

Euphoria

You might argue that euphoria is good, yes, it is good. But when it is related to the Forex market, it becomes dangerous. For example, if a trader wins a few profitable traders, he or she might become confident when trading the next trade. Well, it is good to feel confident when entering the next trade, but feeling overly confident is not a good thing. When traders become overly confident, they don't watch or study the market as they did before. The consecutive profitable trades should not get into your mind and increase the level of confidence. When trading Forex if you are overconfident, you will not be able to accept the loss if the trade doesn't react the way you wanted. Hence, it is better to remain calm even if you make profits continuously.

Fear

Most traders who enter the market with no knowledge about trading tend to fear the market. Also, some traders might fear because they cannot effectively trade using any specific strategy. However, usually, when a trader continuously experiences losses, he or she may tend to fear to trade. Perhaps, it is understandable because losing hard-earned money isn't easy. But, you can avoid the mistake of risking more than the amount that you are comfortable with. Most naïve traders don't follow this rule even if we keep repeating it. If fear persists, you will not be able to trade better trades or become successful. It has the power to keep you away from good trades as well. Hence, try to overcome fear by limiting the amount you risk in trading. For the naïve traders, start your journey on a demo account without directly entering the live account. If you do so, you'll be able to learn to control emotions.

Greed

You might have heard that people say only bulls and bears make money, but pigs get slaughtered. If you don't understand what it means, it means greed. If you are greedy, you will not be able to make money in the market. Instead, you will be kicked out of the market. Mostly, traders become greedy when they don't have self-discipline. Most traders make quick decisions when the market shows profitable trade signals, but it is not recommended. Instead, you must be calm and collected. Take some time to understand the market, focus on the risk ratio, set a plan, and then enter into the trade. Also, remember, if you are risking more than what you are ready to lose, it apparently shows your level of greed to make money. Thus, you must overcome greed if you don't want to lose your account.

Revenge

This is one of the funny behaviors of traders because what is the point in revenging the market? For the Forex market, you are just one amongst the millions, and it doesn't make sense. However, if you are trying to revenge trade just because you lost a few trades, remember, this might lead to further losses. When you are emotional, you will not be able to make wise decisions. Hence, you must wait for some time until your mind is stable and ready to trade.

So, when learning the psychology of trading, you might find it exciting. But, success can decide when you take these things into practice. You don't have to try these tips and ideas on the live account, instead use the demo account. The Forex market is one of the best markets because it has provided solutions for almost all the issues. So, as traders, if you solve your personal trading issues, you will be able to become a successful trader.

MASS PSYCHOLOGY AND ITS MEASURES

Following are a list of things required for becoming a successful Forex trader

Trading plan: A forex trader should have a trading plan that should be prepared well in advance. The trading plan should list out his entry and exit conditions as well as his money management rules. This is of utmost importance and he should religiously follow his trading plan to the tee. In order to become a successful forex trader, he should never deviate from the trading plan.

Discipline: This is one of the most important qualities needed to be a successful forex trader. A trader should be disciplined and methodical in the way he goes about with forex trading. He should not only meticulously plan his trading, but should also be disciplined enough to follow it.

Ability to do analysis: A forex trader should have the ability to analyze the technical charts and other financial data in order to become a successful forex trader. He should invest in himself and learn how to use the financial tools that would help in becoming a better trader. Trading is a very competitive job and one needs to be always one step ahead of others in order to be successful.

Emotional stability: It is very important to keep emotions and trading separate. In order to be successful, the trader should be able to trade like a machine and not let emotions affect his trades. He shouldn't let losses affect him nor should he get overly excited about the winning trades.

Hard work: Nothing beats hard work for becoming a successful forex trader. The trader should be prepared to put in a lot of hours and research the forex market thoroughly before each trading day. Most successful forex traders have a pre-trading session wherein they analyze the global markets, check charts, read various financial newspapers, note down key economic events of the day etc. before they start their trades.

Good knowledge of charting and analysis tools: In order to be a successful forex trader, it is very important to have good knowledge on the usage of charting and other analytic software. The usage of these trading software's raises the odds of success considerably, so it is important to have a good understanding of them.

Constant Learning: Trading field requires constant learning. The trader should be prepared to learn throughout his trading career. Something that might work now might not work after 5 years. So it's very important to constantly adapt and keep learning in order to be a step ahead of others. A good trader should be on the constant look out of learning new things that might help him with his trading be it the usage of a trading software or a new way of analysis.

Mastering fear: It is very important to master fear in order to be a successful forex trader. The trader should be prepared to take losses now and again and should understand that it's a part and parcel of the game. The inability to book losses and holding on to a losing position can result in more losses. The trader should also be ready to take a trade when a good opportunity arises and should not allow fear to hold him back.

Thinking on your own: It is very important to think on your own and make trading decisions and to not just blindly follow the crowd. As the saying goes, "buy into the fear and sell into the greed!" Now, this does not mean to always do the opposite to what others do. It just means that the trader should have an open mind and should have the ability to think on his own and make decisions accordingly.

Awareness of the global events: Forex markets are affected by the major international events that occur. So it's important to have an understanding of the key economic events happening globally as the forex markets are traded globally and affected by these economic events. A few examples of the key economic events are Federal Bank interest rate decision, ECB rate decision, GDP data of key economies, job data of key economies, inflation data of key economies etc.

Never blame the market: The market might behave irrationally but the trader should be responsible for reading the market cues and making trading decisions. Instead of playing the blame game he should learn from each mistake and learn from it. The trader should understand the risks associated with trading and have a proper money management rule in place.

Trading journal: It is important to maintain a trading journal and make an entry of all the trades he makes. The reasons for taking that particular trade should also be noted down. This would help in analyzing the trades later and help in avoiding the mistakes made. This would also help in identifying the good trades made and look for similar patterns later on.

Choosing the right broker: It is important to choose the right broker. Some of the factors that should be considered while selecting a broker should be a) low brokerage b) fast and reliable trading terminal c) ease of trading and good research and charting software's that the broker provides.

Money management rules: This is perhaps the most important among all things that are mentioned till now. A money management rule is basically the rules that define the maximum loss a trader can afford to take per trade or at a point of time. Most forex traders never risk more than 2- 5 % per trade. They also never risk more than 10-20 % at a particular point across all trades. It is very important to follow these rules; else you run the risk of wiping out your entire trading account in a matter of days, if not hours! It is always better to limit your losses and live to fight another day!

Chapter 6: MONEY AND POSITION MANAGEMENT

The most standard system executed in trading is cutting adversities and riding productive positions to ensure that mishaps are inside reasonable cutoff focuses. This presence of mind procedure joins a position limit, a loss limit, and clear peril. A position limit is the most extraordinary proportion of any money a dealer allows to carry on, at any single time. Whereas, a loss limit is a measure planned to avoid unsustainable setbacks made by traders by means of techniques for setting to stop disaster levels. It is fundamental that you have stop-loss orders in place.

In a clear system, intermediaries use guidelines when attempting to control change scale risk to measure their arranged increments against their possible mishaps. The thinking is that most traders will lose a double indistinguishable number of times from their profits, so a direct guideline for trading is to keep your danger/compensate extent to 1:3.

The idea of a stop loss is to help a trader have a small stop loss and avoid emotions from controlling the decisions you make.

The Risk/ Ration Reward

It is good to have a risk/reward ratio of 1:3 or 1:2. In other words, the trader is ready to risk $2 per share and make $4 per share — a risk/reward ratio of 1:1 means that you can't enter a trade because it is not worth that risk.

For experienced traders, they know where to set a stop loss. You won't find these traders wondering where to place a stop loss. Instead, they are much aware that once they open a trade position, they want the best risk/reward ratio.

When to set stop losses?

The best time for you to set up stop loss is the same time when you place an order. It is always good to know exactly where you should put a stop loss. Don't start to wonder or guess. So once you place an order, you set your stop loss immediately because if you wait, you'll start to worry. Also, when feeling worried, you may end up placing it in the wrong place. That may cost you a lot.

Where to Set Stop Loss

There is no exact answer to this question, but there are some tips to follow when you want to set a stop loss in forex trading. Before you read the tips, here are some of the common mistakes that most traders make.

1. Placing a stop too tight

When you have a close stop loss, chances are that it will be stopped early. The forex market is volatile, and that means that you should not have a very tight stop loss. Traders afraid of losing their money place a close stop loss. As a result, they minimize the potential of losing their money. The trick with a tight stop loss is that you will have a lot of small losses that add up to form a significant loss.

2. Placing a wide stop loss

While a tight stop loss is bad, an extensive stop loss is discouraged. Some traders don't want their stop loss to be reached, and so they place a very wide stop loss. Although it is rare for an extensive stop loss to be activated, when it happens, the loss is even huge.

So what is the best thing to do? You have to go for something that is in between a vast stop loss and a tight stop loss. Take time to monitor the movement in price. When you don't see a trend, don't trade. When the trend is powerful, that should be easy for you to identify the sequence. The most important thing is to monitor the price because it is the best signal to predict a correction.

Placing a Stop Loss below the Last Low

You can still place a stop loss at the last significant low when you are in a long position. When the trend is stable, you should make some profit. But when the trend is weak, you'll be stopped out. That is okay because the price will go lower than the stop loss. The same applies in a downtrend. You could be looking forward to placing your stop loss above the last high.

Set Stop-Loss in a Downtrend

In case the downtrend goes past the previous high, then buyers should attempt to take over the control. You don't want to run short in this case, so you should close your position and look for other opportunities.

Increasing the Stop Loss

Many forex traders don't like to use this technique, yet it is the best. First, you place your stop loss once you open a trade. There are times when you'll get stopped fast, but the trade should continue. However, the most critical point comes when you have a profitable trade position. Can it change and shake your stop loss?

When faced with this situation, increase your stop loss to the entry point. That means if the price goes against your position, you won't lose a single dollar. That leads to another interesting question. When is the right time to increase the stop loss? Well, don't do it immediately when you make a profit. Wait for some time and monitor the trade. You need to master how to play around with your system but in a smart way.

Sometimes, the price may continue to rise when you expect it to drop. In this case, continue to increase your stop loss even further. By increasing your stop loss, you will be protecting your profit. When the price doesn't reach your target, close the trade with the profit that you have made. This is an example of trailing stop loss because the stop loss rises as the price increases. There are other methods that you can use to trail stop loss. That is for you to find out. Remember, it is from trying out that you find the best one to use.

The 1% Rule

Some traders use the 2% rule. The 1% rule requires traders to risk only 1% of their trading capital on any single trading position. However, because of small capital, many traders don't follow this rule. The best thing about this rule is that even when you have ten losing trades, you'll still retain a good percentage of your money. So you can see why you should train yourself to follow the 1% rule. Whether you have $100 in your account or more than $100, learn to use this rule if you don't want to lose all your money. Forex trading can be risky, especially when the market is volatile. Nobody will force you to use this rule, but you should make it a habit of using it in any trade that you open.

When trading with Fibonacci numbers, it is pretty easy to use stop losses. For example, if you want to join a long-term trading position, you must wait until when a correction happens to the retracement line.

Stop loss is a critical topic. Each trader has their way of doing it. So you should also find yours. Create your trading plan and test out different ways of placing a stop loss. You will take time before you discover the best way suitable for you.

Money management tips

Is there a secret to success in forex trading? No. But there are a few things that all successful traders do, and are no secret. You merely have to be smart with money management.

Money management is not a new term in forex. It is just the knowledge and skill you use to manage your Forex trading account. That is the secret to a long successful trading career. Although many traders forget to use it, this section outlines ground rules that you can follow to control your account effectively.

Don't be carried away with making big money. This may cause you to lose a lot of money. There is no easy money in forex trading. To be successful in trading, you must learn to be patient and learn to trade small. Not all trades will give you profits. That is why you should plan on losses.

Another thing that you must do is to risk a small percent of your money on each trade. By doing this, you will reduce the risk of losing all your money. You can risk either 1% or 2% of your money. However, experienced traders go as high as 5%, but not more than that. Remember. It is easy to lose money in forex, but hard to regain.

Use Limit Orders

Successful traders know how to use a stop loss. Stop loss will control how much profit you make. A stop loss order will protect your investment and allow you to make small gains.

The Size of Your Trades

Traders are advised to open small trading positions. One of the reasons for this is because when you have a losing trade, you can decide to open another reverse trade position to compensate your losses.

Learn To Practice with Virtual Money

There is a good reason why the virtual method of trading was invented. Don't ignore it. Test all your trading strategies with virtual money before you start to trade on a real trading account. When you switch to actual trading, don't stop to use a virtual account when you want to test a new strategy. Don't risk your money on a real account that may cause you to lose all your money.

Tip

It is easy to master money management tips, but not easy to stick to it. But if you can discover the best money management methods that work for you, continue to use it and don't be carried away with the greed to make more money.

TRADING JOURNAL

One of the things that seasoned traders will tell you is that, more often than not, trading isn't about finding the secret "recipe" to success. It is mainly about having discipline. We have already seen why discipline plays a vital role in your trades. However, one of the ways that you can maintain discipline is by keeping a record journal. Institutional traders, regardless of their rank and their degree of success are trained to keep a journal until the habit of recording their transactions and other behaviors becomes automatic. The main reason for this was to instill a sense of accountability. After all, these traders are dealing with millions of dollars. How did these traders maintain their journal?

One of the habits that they formed was that for every long and short position that they made, for every stop-loss point they set up, every risk-reward ratio that they decided upon, they had to have a solid rationale for doing so.

It was always, "I am doing this because of the following reasons that are based on large amounts of research and information."

They never decided something without a strong foundation to carry their decisions.

Which is why this level of accountability leads to the formation of some of the best traders in the world. You might think that this is an extreme practice and only pertains to traders who are dealing with large sums of money.

On the contrary, it becomes even more important to you.

Why?

Because you are not dealing with someone else's money. You are using your own money.

For banking traders, they receive a fixed paycheck regardless of how poorly they perform. Of course, repeated mistakes mean that they are asked to leave the job. But in essence, they don't have any personal loss. In your case, forget getting a paycheck. If you lose, you are slowly drying up your own reserves. Additionally, institutional traders have multiple chances to make the money back without disrupting their personal lives. If you experience a loss, then you might find your entire life upended.

Now, your journal is different from the checklist and questions that were created when you were building your trading plan.

Here are some of the things you should include in your journal.

Currency Pair Information

In this section, you are going to make notes about the currency pairs and how you have traded with them. This will work best if you have prepared a table and then taken a print out of the sheet.

Target Trades

In this section, you are going to list all the trades that you are going to make. Essentially, you are waiting for the current trade to generate its results so that you can proceed with your next trade.

Let's say that currently, the date is November 1.

Your entry should look something like this:

November 2

- Buy USD/CAD at 1.1712
- Stop loss placed at 1.1700
- Target 1: 1.1760
- On reaching Target 1, Target 2: 1.1790
- No Target 3. High Risk.

With just a few instructions, you have made your next task easier. You have given yourself clear instructions. The next day, let us assume that you had one of those mornings where you just can't seem to find the energy to even move your pinky.

You force yourself out of bed and realize that you need to get back to trading. However, you are in no mood to think straight. What do you do? How can you keep your trades going? Is this the end of the world?

Wait! There is no need to panic. After all, you have already set a plan into motion. Everything will be okay!

Make sure that by the end of the day, you have taken a small portion of your time to create a plan that will help you the next day.

Completed or Existing Trades

Of course, just like you have planned for future trades, you should also be recording your completed or existing trades. Spend some time looking through the trades you have already made to find out any mistakes you may have made. However, not only can you use this section to identify the losses, you might just discover a trend that you wouldn't have otherwise noticed while looking at the charts.

Think of it this way.

When you are talking with your friend, you might inject your responses and questions with a lot of "uhms" and "ahs". However, do you know how many of these blanks are inserted into one sentence? Are you aware of the frequency of these blanks? If you start recording your conversation and then play it back later, you might be surprised by the results.

Reporters and newscasters often record the way they speak and play it back to themselves so that they can improve their speech patterns. They can identify when they are most likely to pause and where they tend to lose track of the conversation.

In a similar way, you are using your journal to track the "uhms" and "ahs" of your trading. You might not be aware that you are making minor mistakes, but when you look through your journal, you might just be surprised by the frequency at which certain actions slip by your awareness.

RISK MANAGEMENT

On the most basic level, risk in currency trading is the same as trading in any other financial market. The risk is that you'll lose money. But risk comes in many different forms and from many different sources. Sometimes the biggest risks are the ones that you never knew existed.

I believe forewarned is forearmed. In this section, I look at some of the main sources of risk that may not be readily apparent or that are easily overlooked.

Here are some basic risks that are associated with currency trading:

Exchange rate risk

Exchange rate risk is the cause of changes in the value of the currency. It relies upon the effect of relentless and largely precarious moves in the general free market action balance. For the period the representative's position is outstanding, the position is at risk to all esteem changes. This danger can be huge and depends on an accessible perspective of which way the financial models will move reliant on each possible factor that happens (or could happen) at some arbitrary time, anywhere on the planet.

Likewise, in light of the fact that the trading outside of the currency trade market is unregulated as it was before, esteem margin limits are not constrained as they were used traditionally for coordinated rate exchanges. The market moves subjected to key and concentrated components progressively.

Interest rate risk

Credit charge risk or interest rate risk suggests the advantage and adversity delivered by instabilities in the forward spreads, closed by forwarding total perplexes and maturity gaps among trades in the currency trade book. This danger is significant to money swaps, forward outright, destinies, and alternatives. To restrain financing cost risk, one should set confines on the hard and fast size of confounds. An ordinary strategy is to detach the mismatches, in perspective of their advancement dates, in up to a half-year and ongoing months. All of the trades are entered in automated systems in order to figure the circumstances for all of the dates of the movement, increments, and hardships. Steady examination of the advance cost condition is vital to check any movements that may influence on the exceptional openings.

Credit risk

Credit risk insinuates the probability that a remarkable money position is not to be repaid as agreed, in view of conscious or programmed action by a counter-party. Credit risk is usually something that is the stress of associations and banks. For the individual representative (trading margin), credit chance is very low as this, and it furthermore stays consistent for associations selected in and overseen by the specialists in European countries. Starting late, the National Prospects Association (NFA) has borne witness to their ward over the currency trade market promotions in the US and continue making a move against unregistered currency trade firms.

The known types of credit risk are as follows:

Substitution Risk

This occurs when counter-gatherings of a fizzled bank or currency trade agent discovers that they are in danger of not getting their assets from the fizzled bank.

Settlement Risk

This occurs in perspective of the diversification of time zones on different territories. In this manner, money related measures are traded at different expenses at different events in the midst of the trading day. Australian and New Zealand Dollars are credited first, then the Japanese Yen, trailed by the European money related measures and then fulfillment with the US Dollar. Thus, payment should be made to a party that will report liquidation or be broadcast obligated, before that party executing its own special portions.

In credit risk, the specialist must consider not simply the market estimation of their money portfolios, but also the potential introduction of these portfolios.

The potential presentation is to be determined by probability examination over the time to maturity of the phenomenal position. The electronic structures directly available are useful in realizing credit chance game plans. Credit lines are successfully checked. In addition, intermediaries for recognition of technique execution use the planning structures introduced in foreign exchange since April 1993. Intermediaries input the hard and fast credit augmentation for a specific counter-party. In the midst of the trading session, the credit expansion is thus adjusted. If the line is totally used, the system will keep the merchant from further dealing with that counter-party. After improvement, the credit line comes back to its one of a kind measurement.

Counter-party default risk

The danger that the principals with a trader, the intermediary's bank, or currency trade market, or the counter-parties with which the bank or currency market trades, will be not capable or will decrease to execute concerning such contracts.

In addition, principals in the spot and forward business divisions have no duty to continue making markets in the spot and forward contracts that are traded.

The budgetary dissatisfaction of counter-get-together could result in significant incidents. Yet again, while trading outside financial structures on an OTC introduce, the trader or customer will oversee associations as principals and establishments may be at risk to setbacks or liquidation. In case of any bankruptcy or mishap, the trader can recover, even in respect to property underlying under his or her record. For example only a certain amount of his traded currency will be handed over to the counter-party.

This particular section of a trader are handled by FCM (Futures Commission Merchant) to confirm that exchange-traded prospects will be subjected to the confined regulatory confirmations overseen by the client segregation rules and procedures.

Country and Liquidity Risk

The liquidity of OTC currency trade will be significantly more noticeable than that of exchange-traded cash in the future. However, the non-exchangeable scenario is seen, especially outside of US and European trading hours.

Additionally, a couple of nations or social occasions of nations have in the past constrained trading limits or repressions on the total expense on currency trading.

Remote exchange rates may vary in the midst of a given time period. The volume which may be traded using certain limitations for trading on positions is believed to produce absolute margin after some time.

Such cutoff focuses may shield trades from execution in the midst of a given trading period. Such impediments or cutoff focuses could keep a trader from a split-second trading in unfavorable positions and subsequently could uncover the specialist's record to liberal adversities.

Additionally, even in circumstances where Foreign Exchange costs have not ended up being subject to managerial restrictions, the General Assistant may be not capable to execute trades at great expenses if the liquidity of the market is not acceptable. It is also useful for a nation or social occasion of nations to constrain the trading of financial guidelines across over national edges. Suspend or bind the exchange or trading of particular money, issue very new fiscal principles to dislodge old ones, mastermind snappy reimbursement of particular cash duties, or demand that trading particular cash could be coordinated for liquidation in a manner of speaking. OTC currency is traded on different non-US markets, which may be liberally more slanted to times of non-liquidity than the Bound-together States promotes in view of a combination of components.

Besides, even where stop setback or limit orders are set up to undertake to compel incidents, these solicitations may not be executable in very frozen state exhibits or may be filled at unforeseeable repulsive esteem levels where non-liquidity or unprecedented shakiness keep them inexorably for great execution.

Marginal Risk

Low edge stocks or currency trade guarantees are typically required in currency trade, (similarly likewise with directed item prospects). These edge approaches allow a high level of use. As needs are, a moderately little value development in an agreement may result in prompt and generous misfortunes in an overabundance of the sum contributed. For instance, if at the season of procurement, 10% of the cost of an agreement were saved as edge, a 10% decline in the cost of the agreement would, on the off chance that the agreement was finished off, result in a complete loss of the edge store before any derivation for business commissions.

A decline of over 10% would result in an all-out loss of the edge stock. A few merchants may choose to submit up to 100% of their record resources for edge or guarantee for foreign trade. Brokers ought to know that the forceful utilization of use will build misfortunes amid times of troublesome execution.

Transactional Danger

Errors in the correspondence when dealing with a merchant's demands may result in startling mishaps. Routinely, even where an out trade is liberally the fault of the overseeing counter-party establishment, the customer's arrangement of activity may be obliged in searching for compensation for coming about setbacks in the record.

Risk of Run

Indeed, even where a dealer/client's medium to long-term perspective of the market might be eventually right, the merchant will most likely be unable to monetarily shoulder momentary hidden misfortunes, and may finish off a situation at a misfortune basically in light of the fact that the individual can't meet an edge call or generally continue such positions. In this manner, even where a dealer's perspective of the market is right, and a cash position may at last pivot and wind up as productive, merchants with inadequate capital may encounter misfortunes.

Chapter 7: CURRENCY FUTURES AND CRYPTOCURRENCIES

WHAT ARE CURRENCY FUTURES?

Future contracts are standardized contracts that are exchanged on organized future markets for the required delivery date. It is generally used by MNEs as a dodging instrument.

The forward contract does not have parcel estimate and is custom-made to the need of the exporter, though the future has standardized round parts. The date of conveyance in forward contracts is debatable, while future contracts are for specific conveyance dates.

The agreement cost in forwarding contracts is based on the offer or the offer spread, while brokerage fees will be charged for the future exchange. The settlement of forwarding contracts is to be done just on the termination date, while benefits or misfortunes are paid day by day if there should be an occurrence of outcomes at the end of the exchange. Forward contracts are issued by business banks though worldwide money related markets (for instance, the Chicago Commercial Trade) or foreign trades issue future contracts.

Swap

Foreign trade swap represents about 55.6 percent of the normal every day foreign trade turnover of the world, while spot bargains represent 32.6 percent and mostly forward for 11.7 percent.

Purchasing cash at a lower rate in one market for quick resale at a higher rate in another with a goal to make benefit from the disparity in return rates in various currency markets is known as currency arbitrage.

Options

Foreign currency trade options provide the owner the right to buy and sell a static amount of foreign money at a pre-determined price, within a specific period. It is an agreement provided by the buyer and that gives the buyer an entitlement but not an responsibility to buy or sell financial assets at a time through a specified date.

The buyer is under no obligation to buy or sell the currency but the seller is required to fulfill their obligation. It provides flexibility for the holder of foreign currency not to buy or sell the foreign currency at pre-determined value unlike a future contract if it is not profitable for the seller.

Currency trade options, are specified in two types, call option and foreign currency options. A call option gives the buyer the right to buy the foreign currency at a pre-determined price and used as future payables. It gives the buyer the right to sell foreign currency at a pre-determined price, and it is used to verge future receivables. However, foreign currency trading options are one of the most effective tools against the exchange rate risks as they offer great flexibility than forward or future contracts because no commitment is required from the buyer under its currency options.

Remember greed is a curse. This is perhaps the perfect advice for forex traders. Any story you might have heard is either false or a pure stroke of luck. Getting greedy can cause you to risk a very big portion of your capital, so no currency trade professional would recommend it. You must not forget that no one gets rich overnight.

CRYPTOCURRENCIES

Many have wondered exactly how cryptocurrency works. As mentioned earlier, cryptocurrency is synonymous with digital currency. It is a decentralized digital coin that functions as a medium of exchange. However, since cryptocurrency is also very different from fiat currency, there is much more to how it works.

A number of the ways cryptocurrencies work are mentioned below:

Transactions: A transaction occurs whenever a cryptocurrency is transferred from a cryptocurrency owner to another via their respective digital wallets. Whenever a transaction occurs, it is automatically submitted to the blockchain, which is a decentralized public ledger where the transaction will be confirmed. After the successful completion of a transaction, it is verified with a **cryptographic signature**, which is an **encrypted cryptography** (security code) for ensuring that the transaction was initiated from a credible source.

The confirmation for a transaction processes within ten minutes. Confirmations are usually accomplished by miners. Once a transaction has been fully confirmed, it will then be added to the public ledger, where it remains for as long as the program exists. A confirmed transaction is thus permanent and can never be altered or deleted from the public ledger.

Public Ledgers: A public ledger is a list of all the transactions that have ever been confirmed and entered into a blockchain. In essence, it is a complete history of a cryptocurrency ever since its creation up to the current moment. The information stored in the public ledger is not limited to a history of transactions alone; it also includes encrypted information about the cryptocurrency owners.

Cryptographic techniques are used to ensure the accuracy of the records that are confirmed and stored in a ledger. One of the benefits of the ledger is the ease for which it can be used to check new transactions to ensure that a digital currency holder does not attempt to spend beyond the number of digital coins he or she possesses. The public ledger is considered synonymous with the term, **transactions**, in blockchain.

Mining: Each transaction must undergo a **confirmation** process before the transaction can be considered to a completed transaction that will then be recorded on a blockchain. This confirmation process is called **mining**. A transaction that has not yet been confirmed can never be recorded in a blockchain, and is thus not considered valid until it is confirmed. It is only after the confirmation of a completed transaction that the transaction can be added to the public ledger. Once the transaction is added to the blockchain, it becomes an irrevocable.

It is important to note that the confirmation process is not easy. It requires that the miners solve difficult computational problems or a mathematical puzzle. Each successful solution the miner makes signals that a transaction has been fully completed.

The confirmation of transactions, however, is not exclusively assigned only to some particular miners. Instead, mining is **open source**, and thus this offers all miners equal opportunities to solve the mathematical puzzles, and therefore confirm transactions.

When a miner has successfully solved a puzzle, he or she then updates the public ledger with a block of transactions. These updated transactions will now be kept permanently in the ledger. The miner receives a fraction of the cryptocurrency as a reward for his or her efforts. This mining process is called a **proof-of-work** system. This is what is responsible for a digital currency's security. The connection between the confirmed transactions, blocks, and the public ledger increases the overall security of the digital currency, thereby making it virtually impossible for an individual to alter the content of the public ledger.

Digital Wallets: Unlike the traditional hard currencies, cryptocurrencies are digital. Cryptocurrencies are thus stored in software programs, known as **digital wallets**, which are digital equivalents of a bank account. Transactions are made when there is a transfer of digital currency from one digital wallet to another. Without digital wallets, no transaction can occur. The recent growth of a vast majority of these coins points to the potential future value they have for everyone's lives.

WHY TRADE WITH CRYPTOCURRENCIES?

The changing perception of cryptocurrency has led to the increased application of these currencies and their use in different aspects of life. A cryptocurrency investor can perform several different kinds of transactions with their coins. Some of these transactions are:

Make a donation: If one wishes to make a donation to a worthy cause or charity organization, this can be accomplished with cryptocurrency. TampaBay.com is the number one platform for cryptocurrency donations.

Finance an education: Some universities around the world accept Bitcoin for tuition. The first university that accepted Bitcoin for tuition was the University of Nicosia, Cyprus. Tuition can also be paid through Bitpay, which is a payment processor with a reputation for excellence. As other universities increasingly begin accepting cryptocurrencies for tuition, it will make this process more convenient for students.

Crowdfunding: When contemplating raising funds for a project, many cryptocurrency investors have now turned to cryptocurrency. Also, as an investor, one can contribute to a project by making a contribution with cryptocurrency. There are several successful projects that have been exclusively funded with digital currencies. For example, the Jamaican Bobsled team was exclusively sponsored by Dogecoin. Another project that was financed exclusively with cryptocurrency is Lighthouse. Cryptocurrency has a bright future as a dependable source of crowdfunding.

Vehicle Purchase: Tesla made the decision to accept payment with Bitcoin and sold the Tesla Model S for a whopping 91.4 Bitcoin. After this successful transaction, another car, a Lamborghini Gallardo, followed suit and was sold for an incredible 216.8 Bitcoin.

House Purchase: The first home bought with digital currency was a villa sold in February, 2014, for 1,000

BTC, in Indonesia. Another home was sold in Las Vegas, Nevada, for a whopping $157,000 BTC.

These are only some of the transactions that can be made with digital currencies. As the number of cryptocurrency enthusiasts grow, the types of transactions that can be made will also increase.

HOW TO TRADE CRYPTOCURRENCIES

Investing in cryptocurrency need not be a chore; it should be viewed instead as an opportunity to see an investment grow. The following tips are designed to help investors make the best decisions when choosing which cryptocurrency to invest in and which platform, or exchange, to use:

- Never invest more than what one can afford to lose. Cryptocurrencies are volatile, fluctuate rapidly, and an investor must be ready for the risks involved. Therefore, to minimize the impact of any loss, one should only invest amounts that will not overly affect their overall finances.

- Make certain that coins are safe. An investor should choose a method of storage they trust and are comfortable with. Many investors prefer the hardware wallet option because of the freedom it offers them to be in absolute control of their currencies.
- Buy cryptocurrencies only from exchanges with excellent reputations. There are many scammers are out there who are ready to prey on the ignorance of newbie investors. Search the ratings of the exchanges first before using them, or use the list of credible exchange platforms above.
- Understand how cryptocurrencies work before investing. This means performing due diligence on these currencies before investing.

How to Invest

While one does not need to understand all the technicalities behind the operation of a cryptocurrency before becoming an investor, this does not mean it is fine just to go ahead and invest in any currency. Before investing in a cryptocurrency, one **must** perform the following:

Due diligence: It is imperative to research the top cryptocurrencies to understand the investment pattern. Research should include the history, current price, rate of appreciation in recent times, and the potential for growth. One can start by researching the top cryptocurrencies discussed above.

Visit an exchange: Pick one of the cryptocurrency exchange platforms from those provided above. Visit the official website of the exchange and create a personal wallet.

Determine how much to invest: Despite the allure of cryptocurrencies and the hype surrounding them, many financial experts have suggested that investors in digital currencies should invest only what they can afford to lose, in the event of circumstances that cause a loss of the investment. In this case, an investor would not lose all their savings but only a portion of it.

Make a purchase: After deciding on an amount to invest, go ahead and buy the currency. There are tons of trusted sellers to buy from. Contact a credible exchange where the chances of getting legitimate coins for purchase are high. Buy the coins and keep them until they appreciate. Later, if desired, sell them for a profit.

If one implements these tips to invest in a cryptocurrency, the investment process should be easy.

BEST CRYPTOCURRENCIES FOR TRADING

Cryptocurrency is an Internet invention that is quickly becoming an international sensation. While Bitcoin continues to be the front runner, thousands of other cryptocurrencies have been created to serve different purposes. Cryptocurrencies, however, are not created equal and each one can have many different features designed to make them stand out from the pack. What follows is a list of the Top Ten Cryptocurrencies that are changing the world:

1. Bitcoin

Bitcoin is the first decentralized digital currency. It is responsible for starting the cryptocurrency revolution that eventually led to the creation of thousands of other currencies designed to meet the growing demand for digital coins. Created by Satoshi Nakamoto in 2009, Bitcoin currently has the biggest capitalization of all the digital currencies in existence. With a market value of approximately $250 billion at the time of this writing, Bitcoin dwarfs other currencies in the digital currency world.

Thus Bitcoin is considered to be the reference point, when discussing cryptocurrencies, because of its importance in relation to other cryptocurrencies. The coin has such a large reputation and value that, in relation to Bitcoin, all other coins are collectively referred to as "altcoins," in other words, alternative coins to Bitcoin. For this reason, Bitcoin always comes up whenever a list of the top cryptocurrencies is compiled.

2. Ether

Created by a 21-year-old programmer, Vitalik Buterin, Ethereum is a decentralized platform that can be used for the execution of smart contracts. First launched in 2015, it was sold to the general public as the "next generation cryptocurrency and decentralized application platform." Currently, as of this writing, Ethereum has an impressive market capitalization of over $73 billion.

Ethereum is known in particular for its peer-to-peer smart contracts that have enabled developers to develop applications that can be used for signing contracts, while making obeisance to the terms of the contract, without a third-party in the middle.

3. Litecoin

In 2011, a former Google employee, Charles Lee, invented Litecoin. He released the digital currency in October 2011 as another alternative to Bitcoin. Litecoin possesses some of the outstanding qualities of Bitcoin, as it can be used both as currency and a medium of exchange. As of this writing, it currently has an estimated market capitalization of $180 million and is gradually working its way to becoming one of the digital currencies that will shape the future.

4. Monero

In 2014, Monero, an open-source digital currency was created. Monero focuses on decentralization, privacy, and scalability. This cryptocurrency can run on a wide range of Operating Systems, such as Linux, Windows, Android, and MacOS. While Monero functions on similar principles as other cryptocurrencies, this digital currency was created with the goal of improving existing digital coins by creating a more egalitarian mining process.

In 2016, the cryptocurrency experienced an unprecedented surge in its market capitalization. Its transaction volume for that year also increased tremendously as a result of the adoption of the currency by some major organizations, such as AlphaBay.

5. Ripple

Ripple is simply one of the best cryptocurrencies on the market. Released to the cryptocurrency market in 2012 as a currency exchange, Ripple is a real-time gross settlement system and remittance network. As of this writing, Ripple currently has a market capitalization estimated to be over $76 million, after it overtook Ethereum to become one of the most sought-after cryptocurrencies. This year alone, Ripple has experienced an astounding 20,000 percent appreciation in value.

Ripple is built on a consensus ledger, internet protocol, and native cryptocurrency. It was designed to make it possible for cryptocurrency users to conduct instant and secure financial transactions with another party anywhere in the world. According to Brad Garlinghouse, Ripple Chief Executive Officer, during an interview with Bloomberg Television, "within the year of crypto, Ripple has outperformed every other digital asset out there."

As a leading cryptocurrency, some banks have integrated the cryptocurrency into their system to make payment easy for their customers. Some of the notable companies that are using Ripple are UBS, UniCredit, and Santander. Many banks and other financial institutions are increasingly adopting Ripple as a credible payment network. Two of the features of this coin that makes it acceptable for use in the banking industry are its affordable price and peerless security.

6. Dogecoin

Dogecoin was not created as a digital currency given the potential to have any impact on people. Instead, it was created as a "joke currency," in the likeness of an Internet meme, Doge. However, the coin took off and gradually triggered the creation of an online community of users. From December 6, 2013, to January 2014, Dogecoin reached an estimated market capitalization of approximately $60 million. Currently, its capitalization is estimated to be $1 billion.

When compared with other digital currencies, the initial production schedule of Dogecoin was rapid. By mid-2015, Dogecoin had 100 billion coins in circulation. Every year since 2015, over 5.2 billion coins have been added. Dogecoin has proven useful in social media, where it is often used for tipping users that contribute noteworthy content to the Internet. Users of this digital currency believe the coin will soon experience a great increase in value, an overall rise in value of the coin that is referred to with the expression "To the moon!"

Dogecoin is also frequently used for fund raising. For instance, during the Doge4Water campaign, it raised thousands of dollars. The campaign was so successful that over 4,000 donors made donations with the coin, including an anonymous donator, who donated some 14 million Dogecoin, worth approximately $11,000 at the time of the donation.

7. Dash

Dash is a cryptocurrency used for making instant, anonymous payments when shopping online. With Dash, purchases from office or home can be made with a direct payment from a Dash wallet. Dash can save time while shopping because the platform makes payments easy and stress-free. While the Dash platform makes payments easy, it also offers a practical way to protect financial information while shopping online. It does this by ensuring that account balances and transaction activities are all kept private.

This privacy additionally helps thwart potential scammers.

Apart from the privacy offered by the platform, Dash also provides maximum security. All the transactions conducted on the platform are confirmed by a very powerful computing power, a 200 TerraHash, and the more than 4,500 servers hosted in strategic locations around the world. All these features make Dash one of the Top Ten Cryptocurrencies to consider investing in to reap many financial benefits from the cryptocurrency world. As of this writing, Dash currently has a market capitalization of approximately $4 billion.

8. MaidSafeCoin

MaidSafeCoin is also known as Safecoin. This cryptocurrency was created by the Secure Access for Everyone (SAFE) network. SAFE is a security-oriented data platform and was created to loan out a space on your personal computer in return for coin. Safecoin is designed to ensure that at there will always be only 4.3 billion coins in circulation. These coins will also never be identical, as the coin has its own unique features and identity. A couple of decentralized apps currently depend on the SAFE network for their data storage because of the security it offers them. As of this writing, the coin has a market capitalization of approximately $40 million.

9. Lisk

Lisk is a unique cryptocurrency, in that it is a crowdfunded digital currency and prides itself as "the first modular cryptocurrency utilizing sidechains." Lisk shares some similarities with Ethereum, such as it can also be used for developing decentralized apps. This is available for developers that are good at Javascript. The currency is useful for creating e-commerce stores, social media platforms, and other decentralized applications. Recognized as the first cryptocurrency built on sidechains technology, as of this writing, it has an estimated market capitalization of $25 million.

10. Zcash

Zcash is another cryptocurrency that is a decentralized and open-sourced. Therefore, it offers privacy protections that cannot be easily breached. This makes it one of the most secure cryptocurrencies. The identities of parties involved in Zcash transactions are carefully concealed when transacting with Zcash, thus hiding information about the recipient, sender, as well as the value of the Zcash held on the blockchain. While Bitcoin remains the undisputed top digital currency, these other nine cryptocurrencies are important competitors in terms of both security and privacy.

Chapter 8:INFORMATION ON RISK

Currency risk refers to the exposure looked by financial specialists or associations that work across over different countries, about an irregular increase or decrease due to the changes in the estimation of one currency in association with another currency.

When a person goes long on EUR/USD, for example, he thinks that the value of the Euro will increase relative to the U.S Dollar. Likewise, with any investment, a person's guess could be wrong and the trade could move against him. While trading in the currency markets, this could be the most obvious risk for a person. He could experience an additional risk by trading less popular currency pairs and by getting into a situation where the transaction itself is shaky, only because he hasn't properly arranged his margin account or haven't chosen a reliable broker or a trading exchange.

It is beneficial to do research of a vast portion of the currency market's trades by banks and not by individuals. They are using currency trade to overcome the threat of currency fluctuations. The currency trade market is using complex algorithms in their computerized trading systems to handle some of the threats. As an individual, you are a less target to many of the threats, and others can be restricted through sound trade management. Any investment, which offers a possible advantage, also has an obstacle, to the point of losing more than the value of a person's trade while trading on margin. This book will help you grasp the risks so your trading is viable.

How to manage risks in currency trade?

Realizing how to deal with and oversee risk is similarly as critical as any examination for making benefits. Have a decent comprehension of risk in the currency trade market. There are different risks that affect the currency trade markets, and some of them are as mentioned. By knowing how these dangers could affect your exchanges, you will be all around to settle on great exchanging choices.

End your misfortunes through stop-misfortune orders. Do not hold on to perceive how the exchange turns in the wake of putting in such a request since it can influence your exchanging diversion. Use low influences. High influences give chances to make amazing benefits, however, recollect that they likewise convey the potential for overwhelming misfortunes.

Know your flexibility for risk. How much risk one can endure differs from one merchant to the next. Before putting an exchange, make this inquiry, "would I be able to bear the loss of this exchange or will I be worried about the misfortune?" Having a certain answer can assist you to stay focused and to abstain from losing profits in your exchanges. Without a doubt, there will be times when you will lose a few or the greater part of your exchanges. This ought to be an impetus to cut down the window ornament on currency exchanging but instead an inspiration to change and enhance your exchanging style and methodologies. Tolerating the worst conceivable result in advance is a decent attribute of effective merchants.

Test any exchanging procedure first before applying it. You can go through demo accounts. Keep feelings under control. Trade dependent on feelings results in misfortunes most of the time due to miscalculated moves. Rather, you need to assume the responsibility of your feelings to refrain from committing senseless errors.

You can have the best currency market on the planet. However, without a strong currency trading strategy, you could lose everything.

Sadly, numerous dealers neglect to execute these measures. Why? Primarily in light of the fact that they appreciate seeking after oodles of cash by making hazardous ventures using influence - in spite of the high possibility that they might all of a sudden lose everything.

Keeping in mind that numerous merchants have had achievements rehearsing these exchanges with demo accounts, they are careless and helpless to succeed in executing such moves without a doubt. Mindful brokers avoid potential risk. Knowing when to cut your misfortunes on exchanges is a hazard-control strategy. This should be possible with a "hard stop", where you use exchanging stage innovation to secure a misfortune stop at a specific dimension, or this should be possible with a "psychological stop", where you mentally choose to restrict the draw-down you are willing to go up against an exchange - making a guarantee to yourself to escape at one point. With either technique, it is vital to fight the temptation to move your misfortune stop to a more distant and more remote point, as speculation esteems decay.

Intermediary commercials influence it to appear to be possible to open a record with $300 and utilize 200:1 use to encourage smaller than usual parcel exchanges of 10,000 dollars, at that point multiplying your cash in a solitary exchange. In any case, this is profoundly risky and stupid. With regard to at first deciding your parcel measure, it's best for new financial specialists to begin from little to consider more prominent adaptability in managing trades.

While using decreased currency rate, estimates are something to be grateful for, as opening numerous parts with money sets could handicap you. For instance, in the event that you go short on EUR/USD and long on USD/CHF, you are presenting multiple times to the USD. What's more, if the USD tumbles, you will endure a two-fold portion of agony. Yet, keeping your general introduction constrained can decrease your risk and increase your prospects for long-haul achievement.

Tools and tips for risk management

Most people in the currency trade markets go for fancy techniques right from the start. However, they neglect very crucial aspects i.e. money or risk management. The fact of the matter is that every trader needs to understand the effectiveness of money and risk management. One should broaden their chances of success, but it should not come with the fact of losing the money or strategic mismanagement.

This book sheds light upon the four principle procedures to oversee risk management.

Forward contracts

A forward contract is a pledge to purchase or move a particular measure of foreign money after a few days or inside a particular time span and at an exchange scale stipulated when the transaction is done. The conveyance or receipt of the money happens on the agreed forward assessment date.

A forward contract cannot be called off. , it can be shut by the repurchase or clearance of the foreign money amount on the desired date and is initially settled upon. Any resultant additions or misfortunes are acknowledged on this date.

For the most part, there is a variety in the forward cost and spot cost of money. On the off chance that the forward is expensive than the spot value, a forward premium is utilized but if the forward cost is lower, a forward discount is utilized.

To process the yearly rate premium or equation, the following equation can be utilized:

Forward premium or discount = (Forward rate − Spot rate)/Spot rate x 360/Number of days under the forward contract

In the formula given above, the conversion scale is communicated as domestic cash units per unit of foreign money. To show, if the spot cost of 1 US dollar is Indian rupees 39.3750 on a given date and its 180-day forward cost cited is Indian rupees 39.8350, the annualized forward premium works out to be 0.92, as under:

Forward premium or markdown = (39.8350 − 39.3750) * 360/180 = 0.92

The forward differential is known as the swap rate. By including the premium (in focuses) to or subtracting the discounts (in focuses) from the spot rate, the swap rate will be changed to an outright rate.

In the event that money with higher loan costs is sold forward, seller appreciates the benefit of clutching the higher procuring cash amid the period between agreeing upon the exchange and its development.

Buyers are off guard since they should hold up until they can acquire the higher-earning cash. The financing cost inconvenience is offset by the forward discount. In the forward market, currencies are getting bought and sold for future facilities, usually for a month, three months, a half year, or much more from the date of exchange.

Conclusion

The forex market is a complex world, and everyone is trying to look for the goose that lays the golden egg. In this case, we are talking about that one trade that will simply propel someone to new heights.

People imagine that getting into the forex market is easy, that pretty soon they will be diving into cash the way Scrooge McDuck takes a joyful dive in his pile of gold coins.

That rarely happens. But the prospect of making some incredible profits still exists, provided you are ready to navigate the complexities of the forex market.

In fact, here is something you should know.

This is a real market. It is the largest financial market in the world, and you have to treat it as such. You can trade this market part-time, or you can do it every day. In fact, you can make it your business—the business of trading.

People have actually quit their day jobs to get into the world of forex trading. However, that is something that you should not even consider if you are starting out. Do not make rash decisions in the hope that you are going to master the markets and strike rich in no time. Those are wonderful ambitions but are not backed by experience.

You see, trading can be learned, of course, but the experience can't be transmitted.

It has to be constructed by every individual through a personal effort of understanding and hard work.

Another thing that is important to understand is that you will never ever stop learning. Markets are changing every day, and the forex is a living organism that evolves in the same way as all its traders. Always remember that although it seems to be an unknown entity, at the end of the day, the market is merely made up of investors, large and small, from all corners of the world, each with his or her own emotions, psychology, and predictable behaviors and reactions.

Do you ever walk up to a doctor and ask him or her if there is a shortcut to reaching where he or she has reached? Would you do that to an engineer or a renowned sportsperson? These people have developed their skills over time. They have honed their abilities as much as possible before they could use them fluently.

It is the same with the forex market. You might need to put in your efforts to learn the tricks of the trade (no pun intended).

Learn to move on after losses. Don't dwell on missed trades or missed pips after you decide to close. There will be hundreds of opportunities in the future. Follow your plan, and follow your system. Practice every day, and experience will come with time, patience, and discipline. Don't look outside for what's already inside. Leave your ego behind; be humble and smart. You can't decide where the market will go, so learn to see where it wants to lead you, not the other way around. Exit bad trades, and hold on to good trades. Set yourself a goal and stop trading when you have reached it.

Lightning Source UK Ltd.
Milton Keynes UK
UKHW020835151220
375245UK00004B/703